IMAGES
of America

WAYNE'S TRACE

FORT DEPOSIT TO FORT INDUSTRY

"The sunset of a century" was also an allegory for the sunset of great Indian nations in the lower Maumee Valley. General "Mad Anthony" Wayne's victory sealed the fates of many successful farmers, hunters, trappers, and traders. The removal was not complete, however; Native Americans are still well represented among the Lucas County citizenry.

IMAGES
of America

WAYNE'S TRACE

FORT DEPOSIT TO FORT INDUSTRY

Charles M. Jacobs

ARCADIA
PUBLISHING

ISBN 978-0-7385-3212-7

Published by Arcadia Publishing
Charleston, South Carolina

Printed in the United States of America

Library of Congress Catalog Card Number: Applied For.

For all general information contact Arcadia Publishing at:
Telephone 843-853-2070
Fax 843-853-0044
E-Mail sales@arcadiapublishing.com
For customer service and orders:
Toll-Free 1-888-313-2665

Visit us on the Internet at www.arcadiapublishing.com

Dedicated to the Maumee Valley Veterans of all Wars.

"Let each heart grow strong in the remembrance of the past, and in the thought of the inestimable blessings for which they contended."

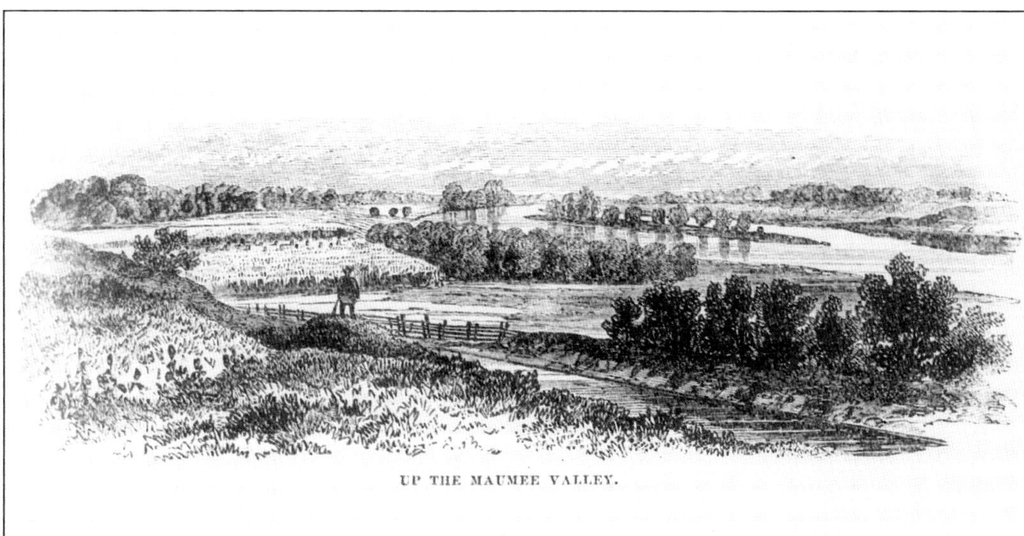

An idyllic vista of the valley, c. 1850. The floodplains, wet woods, and island groves are indicative of the terrain encountered by Wayne's Legion and the Indian Confederacy. (Courtesy of the Center for Archival Collections, Bowling Green State University.)

Contents

ACKNOWLEDGMENTS

Like Wayne's campaign, the book-building process has been a long and arduous trek through a wilderness fraught with peril. I would like to thank all the scouts and soldiers that brought it to a successful conclusion: my wife, Karen Craigo; the staff (Glenna Berres, Pat Hall, Tonya Haynes, and Dianna Stvartak), trustees, and volunteers (especially "Gal Friday" Peg Stephens) of the Lucas County-Maumee Valley Historical Society; William Block, Jr., Mary Mackzum, and all their great and gracious archivists in *The Blade* corporate library; Jim Marshall and his crackerjack crew in the History and Genealogy Department of the Toledo-Lucas County Public Library; Ann Bowers and Paul Yon and their staff at the Center of Archival Collections, Bowling Green State University; Joe Ludwig and his staff at the Maumee Public Library; Barbara Floyd of the Canaday Center, Carlson Library, University of Toledo; the William L. Clements Library at the University of Michigan; the Fort Wayne-Allen County Public Library; the Fallen Timbers Battlefield Preservation Commission; the fine folks of Metroparks of the Toledo Area; Dr. Larry Nelson of Fort Meigs State Memorial; Dr. G. Michael Pratt of Heidelberg College; Winterthur; Doug and Steve Johnson of the Colby Street Irregulars; Daryl Smith of the Historical Miniature Gaming Society, Great Lakes Chapter; *The Maumee Mirror*; the Toledo Community Foundation for their support of the Lucas County-Maumee Valley Historical Society's program "Our Native American Heritage"; and Jeff Ruetsche and his troops at Arcadia Publishing.

INTRODUCTION

"Viewed from the perspective of history, the Battle of Fallen Timbers, like all other battles, was a messy and desperate affair," observed Dr. G. Michael Pratt of Heidelberg College in his keynote address at the bicentennial commemoration of the battle in August 1994. "Like all other battles," the professor of anthropology elaborated, "it was a gamble among political leaders that was wagered with human lives."

Attempting to document Wayne's Trace* from Fort Deposit to Fort Industry at times can be both messy and desperate. The sagas of Fort Industry of Toledo along with Chief Turkey Foot and his boulder, for example, have been dimmed and clouded with the passing of time, and the groping researcher is at a loss to come up with—excuse the pun—"rock solid" history.

What does emerge in towering fashion from the murk is an appreciation for the human lives, those lost in the gamble—rallying on a rock or executed as a deserter—as well as those spared, to go on to become President of the United States or condemned to the "huddled masses" of a refugee camp.

Public appreciation for Wayne's Campaign and the corresponding Native American resistance is growing. Fort Miamis and the Fallen Timbers Battlefield have been finally accorded National Park affiliations. Several prominent historians have gone on record in affirming that the Battle of Fallen Timbers was not only one of our key military engagements, but also, in a broader sense, that the event was a pivotal episode, a watershed, in national and international affairs. A bicentennial celebration and heritage tourism have helped to fuel the interest in the era and events.

The Battle of Fallen Timbers Monument area, with its Wayne Memorial and Turkey Foot Rock, has become a focal point for historical commemorations. The occasional pilgrim wends his or her way to the venerated shrines, and continues a long tradition of leaving an offering, be it a plug of tobacco or a bouquet of flowers.

What remains little understood and appreciated are the rich material and popular culture associated with the subjects. Whether it is a diminutive postage stamp or a towering monument, this culture can speak volumes on history. Perhaps even more so, it can shed light on how people have viewed their history.

Nearly a quarter of a century ago, I fulfilled a youthful dream and accepted a position as Student Conservation Association Representative at what was then known as the Custer Battlefield National Monument. To this day I find the story of Little Big Horn to be intriguing—indeed, exciting. I have found the Battle of Fallen Timbers, as archetypal epic of defeat—and victory—to be equally fascinating. Whereas the Little Big Horn tradition has golden-maned George Custer and his Last Stand Hill, Fallen Timbers has Turkey Foot and his Rock. Whereas the Little Big

Horn tradition has its dynamic Crazy Horse and Sitting Bull, Fallen Timbers has its colorful Blue Jacket and Little Turtle. Now if only Errol Flynn had portrayed "Mad Anthony" Wayne or Anheuser-Busch had printed a "Turkey Foot's Last Fight" . . . .

Charles M. Jacobs

* I preferred this term to "trail," which today most folks associate with a divided highway; I am still bewildered by the fact that so few motorists realize that the modern Anthony Wayne Trail more or less parallels the march of Wayne's Legion in 1794.

One

Contest and Conquest

The western expansion of the United States—and its resultant imperial struggle—began in earnest with the Ordinance of 1787. The federal government's creation of a Northwest Territory, on the heels of the legitimization of the new republic with the Treaty of Paris, exacerbated the already tense situation in the Ohio Country. Land-hungry speculators and settlers saw the indigenous peoples and English trading and military outposts as obstacles to statehood. The Algonquians and their allies faced constant pressure to displace, to cede land and move west . . . or to become a protectorate of the British Empire, and take up arms to resist the advances and incursions. Congress authorized President Washington to secure Northwest interests, and in the fall of 1790 General Josiah Harmar and an army comprised of ill-prepared regulars and militia were repulsed in the upper Maumee Valley by a stalwart defense coordinated by Little Turtle of the Miami.

The setback, coupled with an Indian attack on a pioneer settlement at Big Bottom along the Muskingum River in 1791, prompted Washington to launch another punitive campaign. This time he called upon his old comrade, Author St. Clair, to lead the military expedition to the land of the Miami. Once again, Little Turtle turned the tables. A furious attack near the present Ohio-Indiana state line resulted in the collapse of St. Clair's army. Recalled Adjutant Ebenezer Denny:

> *The men . . . left with few officers, became fearful, despaired of success, gave up the fight, and crowded in the center of the field, and no exertions could put them in any order even for defense; [they were] perfectly ungovernable.*

Washington called it a disaster "too shocking to think of." He affirmed that St. Clair was "worse than a murderer," adding that the curse of heaven was upon the general for losing half his command in the rout. Native American morale was high. The British solidified their hold on the Great Lakes. Dissent and dissatisfaction with Washington and his "inefficient and ineffective" federal policy was growing. The gateway to the Northwest Territory, bloodied by two staggering reverses, remained barred.

Explorers of the Northwest Territory described a "Veritable Eden" with a bounty of natural resources. The "First Frontier" represented the first opportunity for colonization by the young Republic and the planting of government beyond the limits of the United States. However, one major obstacle to the expansion was the fact that the British, the French, and the Native Americans were all well established in the territory.

A clash of cultures was inevitable. The Ohio Country was awash in blood as settlers attacked American Indian villages.

Violence between the cultures became all too common.

Responding to the settlers' attacks, the American Indians launched raids of reprisal.

This drawing shows the mutual fear and lack of understanding that the cultures had for one another.

The contest for the Old Northwest, the Indian Wars of the late 18th century, culminated in the Battle of Fallen Timbers on August 20, 1794, at the Foot of the Rapids, present Monclova and Waynesfield townships, Lucas County, Ohio. General "Mad Anthony" Wayne's victory, which had been preceded by two military debacles orchestrated by Generals Josiah Harmar and Arthur St. Clair, ultimately opened America's "First Frontier" to white settlement and helped legitimize the new federal government while dispossessing Native Americans and disrupting their traditional ways of life.

The Indian Confederacy in the lower Maumee Valley represented one of the greatest Native American aggregates—what General Wayne described as a "Grand Emporium" of "hostile Indians," their farms and villages—ever assembled on the North American continent. In August of 1794, Wayne reported to Secretary of War Henry Knox that "the margin of the beautiful rivers, the Miami of the Lakes (Maumee) and Au Glaize, appear like one continued village for a number above and below this place (Ft. Defiance); nor have I ever before beheld such immense fields of corn in any part of Americas from Canada to Florida."

Two

MEN AT ARMS

The Campaign of 1794 brought together a colorful cast of characters, men at arms who were destined to become the romantic heroes of school textbooks or villains vilified by writers for the popular press. Out of what historian Edward E. Spicer (*A Short History of the Indians of the United States*, 1969) called a "forming and fomenting population of embattled Algonkians from many parts," arose a formidable combination of warrior chiefs. Individually, they would navigate their respective tribes and nations through the tempests of war onward to the pastures of peace; collectively, they would orchestrate would might have represented up until that time the largest Indian confederacy on the North American continent.

The British, who had been doing something of a *do-si-do* with their Indian allies after the American Revolution, put their trust in several diplomats who advocated the creation of a native buffer state north of the Ohio River. Protectors of the lucrative fur trade, they served as "observers" and "advisors" to the Confederacy during Wayne's Campaign.

The United States' unsuccessful overture for peace and a clamor for a sufficient army to carry out the designs of the Northwest Ordinance, to protect the Virginia frontier, and to open the Ohio Country, set in motion what was labeled the "Third Maumee Expedition." In April of 1793, a column of infantry, cavalry, and artillery amassed along the Ohio River began a long yet methodical trek into enemy territory. This juggernaut called the Legion of the United States boasted seasoned veterans of frontier battles, crack troops rigorously and relentlessly drilled in a manual of arms, and officers who would not flinch in battle. The "bravest of the brave," Anthony Wayne, confidently reported from Fort Greenville in October of 1793:

> *The safety of the Western frontiers, the reputation of the legion, the dignity and interest of the nation, all forbid a retrograde maneuver, or giving up one inch of ground we now posses, until the enemy are compelled to sue for peace.*

Anthony Wayne was hand-picked by his comrade George Washington to lead the U.S. Army. The President of the United States was livid when he learned of St. Clair's crushing defeat at the hands of Little Turtle. He feared that General Wayne was "addicted to the bottle," but he realized the very existence of the young government might hinge on the Army's victory or defeat and chose a seasoned veteran who had a reputation for getting the job done.

Wayne's Legion of the United States was composed of relentlessly trained "crack" troops. The martial traditions of Classical Rome, which were reflected in the army's finery, dovetailed with the organizational rigors imposed by "Mad Anthony." *The Road to Fallen Timbers* was authorized by the Department of the Army and released as a poster in 1963.

(*right and bottom, left*) Wayne was respected as "The Wind" and "The Chief Who Does Not Sleep" by his Native American adversaries. Among his men he was regarded as a strict—if not "mad"—taskmaster.

(*bottom, right*) "Apprentice in Arms," Aide-de-Camp William Henry Harrison proposed an order of battle to Wayne. His reputation as a dauntless frontier soldier propelled him into his short-lived (31 days) Presidency of the United States.

Army officer William Clark left a vivid journal of the column's march down the Maumee Valley. He described the Indian Confederacy as a "Hydra" and feared that the Legion might "forego such opportunities of rendering their Country a service," i.e., lopping off Hydra's head. Clark's adventure was a prelude to his overland expedition to the Pacific with Meriwether Lewis. (Courtesy of the Library of Congress.)

Described by a contemporary as "that worst of bad men," James Wilkinson was on the Spanish payroll at the time of Fallen Timbers. The officer was Wayne's sharpest critic and a *bete noire* of the federal government; he was ultimately i mplicated in the Burr Conspiracy. (Courtesy of the W.L. Clements Library, University of Michigan.)

Although several historians have placed the great frontiersman Simon Kenton at the Battle of Fallen Timbers, there is evidence to suggest that he made it no farther than Fort Defiance. Other historians have posited that Kenton, along with his mentor Daniel Boone, provided the models for Natty Bumppo, the celebrated Deerslayer. Novelist James Fenimore Cooper had his protagonist reminisce,

I followed Mad Anthony one season through the beeches;
but there was altogether too much tattooing and regulating
among his troops, so I left him. . . .

William Wells served as Captain of Spies for the Legion. His captivity and upbringing among the Miami gave him valuable insight into Native American warfare, and his reconnaissance of the Foot of the Rapids provided the Legion with a crucial edge in their ensuing clash. Wells was Little Turtle's son-in-law and fought at the Chief's side in the defeat of St. Clair. According to tradition, upon parting company, Wells and his father-in-law agreed to kill one another should they meet in battle.

Little Turtle of the Miami, a seasoned commander and vanquisher of generals Josiah Harmar and Arthur St. Clair, counseled peace with Wayne but was overruled. Nonetheless, he probably took his place in the lines of the Indian Confederacy at the Battle of Fallen Timbers.

That the young Tecumseh participated in the Battle of Fallen Timbers is a subject for debate among historians. There is no doubt, however, that Wayne's campaign strengthened this Shawnee's resolve to resist white expansion and preserve traditional culture.

Portraiture of Tecumseh is equally enigmatic. Here is another impression of the great warrior-chief that appeared in popular histories published in the 19th century.

Described by one contemporary as a "brave masculine figure of a man," Blue Jacket of the Shawnee was a courageous leader but lacked the tactical sagacity of Little Turtle.

REV. BETWEEN-THE-LOGS
Indian Missionary.

Between-the-Logs of the Wyandot was a young participant in the conflict. After Fallen Timbers, he was converted at the mission at Upper Sandusky, Ohio, and became a traveling evangelist.

Tarhe the Crane was 50 or older at the time of battle. This Wyandot leader had a long a distinguished military career on the frontier.

Black Hoof was said to have distinguished himself in battle against both St. Clair and Wayne. The Shawnee leader encouraged his people to adopt many white ways after the Treaty of Greenville.

Alexander McKee, Deputy Superintendent of Indian Affairs for upper Canada, was a leading proponent of British-Native resistance to U.S. expansion. He watched from afar as Wayne's troops routed the Confederacy and destroyed his homes, stores, and crops at the Foot of the Rapids.

John Graves Simcoe, the lieutenant governor of upper Canada, regarded Wayne's Campaign as an affront and menace and took decisive steps to protect the British Crown's lucrative fur-trading interests in the lower Maumee Valley. He ordered the construction of a stronghold at the Foot of the Rapids, Fort Miamis, and directed the emplacement of cannons "of larger caliber than what Mr. Wayne can bring against it."

The Eastern press labeled the Pennsylvanian Simon Girty a loyalist renegade and the "beast" behind the burning at the stake of Colonel William Crawford after the Battle of Sandusky, 1782. Girty's captivity by the Iroquois qualified him as astute mediator between the British and Indians. He was instrumental in bolstering the Native American Confederacy that resisted Wayne's Legion. He took the field as an observer.

Marge Elder, a descendant of Wayne's color-bearer, Captain W.H. Johnson, holds a battle flag said to have been unfurled at Fort Deposit. (Courtesy of *The Blade*, Toledo.)

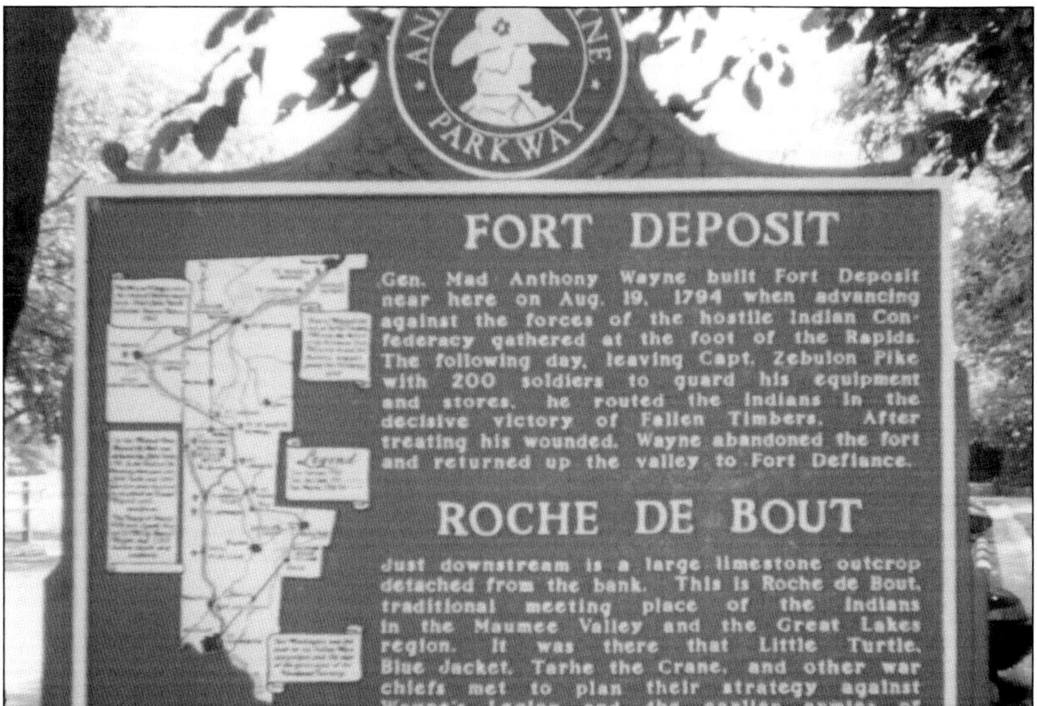

A plaque along a scenic overlook off the Anthony Wayne Trail in Waterville. The interpretive text makes reference to Legion officer Zebulon Pike, a name many Americans came to associate with Western expansion, specifically Pike's Peak.

Three

FORT DEPOSIT

Wayne's army finally broke winter camp at Greenville in July of 1794. Approximately 2,000 strong, the Legion was organized into four sub-legions of infantry: light infantry, riflemen, dragoons, and cannoneers. They were joined by the Kentucky militia, 1,500 mounted men under the command of General Charles Scott. The Legion and militia marched down the Maumee valley, intent on compelling their adversaries to sue for peace—or to run before their bristling bayonets and collapse under their withering fire.

Captain of Spies William Wells and a contingent of scouts preceded the column downstream. They carried a message, an appeal from their commander to the Indians:

> *Brother! Be no longer deceived or led astray by the false promises and language of the bad men at the Foot of the Rapids. They have neither the power nor inclination to protect you. No longer shut your eyes to your true interests and happiness; nor your ears to this overture to peace. But, in pity to your innocent woman and children, come, and prevent further effusion of your blood. Let them experience the kindness and fellowship of the United States of America, and the in-valuable blessings of peace and tranquility.*

The scouts brought back news that the British and the native forces at the Foot of the Rapids, present Maumee and Perrysburg, were well-alerted to the offensive, that they were not cowed by Wayne's resplendent van and were not about to sue for peace; in fact, they were making defensive preparations, if not planning a counter-offensive.

The army continued its forward march along the north bank of the Maumee River, arriving at a place described by historian Clark Waggoner as a "favorite spot favored by the Redmen for hunting and fishing." Waggoner also maintained that here, at *Roche de Bout*, was the "last resting place of nearly 200 Redmen killed not in battle, but in heat of passionate rage." The tribal massacre was said to have begun when an unattended infant fell off the precipice to his death, and escalated to wholesale carnage when the irate husband flung his inattentive wife off the same overlook.

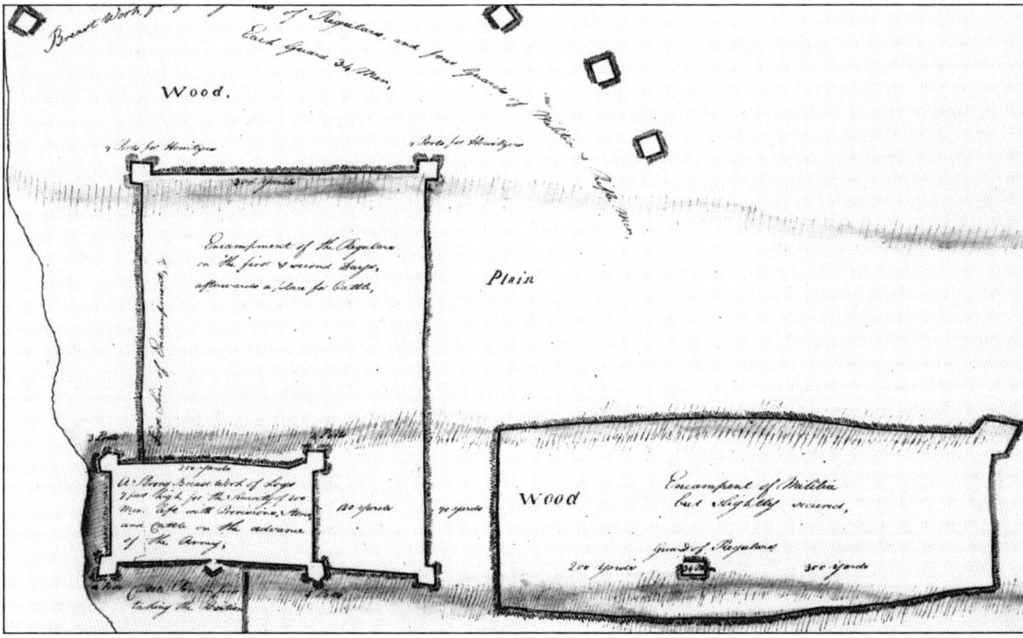

Fort Deposit, as shown in this plat, was a temporary structure with rectangular enclosures, corner bastions, and breastworks for guards, all constructed of logs. The largest of the enclosures measured approximately 650 by 360 yards. An extract from the log of Lieutenant Boyer, U.S. Army, described the activity on the "brow":

> *Camp Deposit—one mile from Grand Oglaize (at Roche de Bout) 18th August, 1794. The legion arrived on this ground, nothing particular taking place. Five of our spies were sent out at 3 p.m. . . . 19 August, 1794—The legion still continued in encampment and are throwing up works to secure and deposit the heavy baggage of the troops, so that the men may be light for action provided the enemy have presumption to favor us with an interview, which if they should think proper to do, the troops are in such high spirits that we will make an easy victory of them . . . ."* (Courtesy of the William L. Clements Library, University of Michigan.)

At Roche de Bout William Clark paused to write, "We behold one of the most beautiful landscapes ever painted." The area was still relatively pristine when this postcard was made in the early 1900s.

Wayne's Legion encamped opposite a landmark described by William Clark as a "small island or craggy rock." Variously named Roche de Beau (handsome or beautiful rock), Roche de Boeuf (beef, ox, or buffalo rock), Roche de Bout (upright or standing rock), and Roche de Boule (bull, bowl, or nut rock), the limestone formation provided the traditional council grounds of the Ottawa and their allies.

More than a century after Wayne's men had felled timber on the bluff opposite Roche de Bout and established Fort Deposit, their clearing was still in evidence.

In 1907 work began on an interurban span on and over Roche de Bout. The local citizenry was outraged and howled that the National Bridge Company was bent on the desecration of one of the most historic sites in the country. (Courtesy of *The Blade*, Toledo.)

Another view of the bridge over the Rouche de Bout. (Courtesy of *The Blade*, Toledo.)

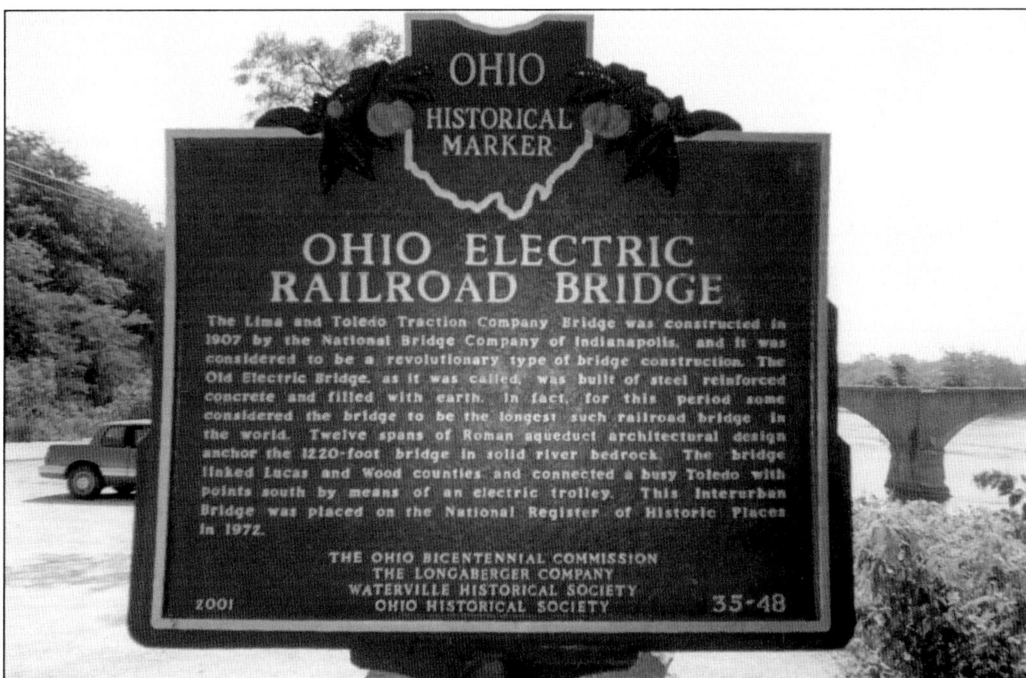

Today an historical marker commemorates the bridge.

The "Roman Aqueduct" fell into disuse and disrepair not long after its completion. Today the ruin provides a scenic vista reminiscent of the Italian countryside. (Courtesy of *The Blade*, Toledo.)

The "Aqueduct" is seen here in its better days. (Courtesy of *The Blade*, Toledo.)

Dresden Howard, seen here standing in front of Richardson's Tavern, near the old fish weirs on the upper rapids, grew up near Roche de Bout and heard what were purported to be eyewitness accounts of the 1794 campaign. He set them down many years later; today, historians question if the memories of the eyewitnesses, and the memory of Howard himself, were not fogged by the passage of time. (Courtesy of the Center for Archival Collections, Bowling Green State University.)

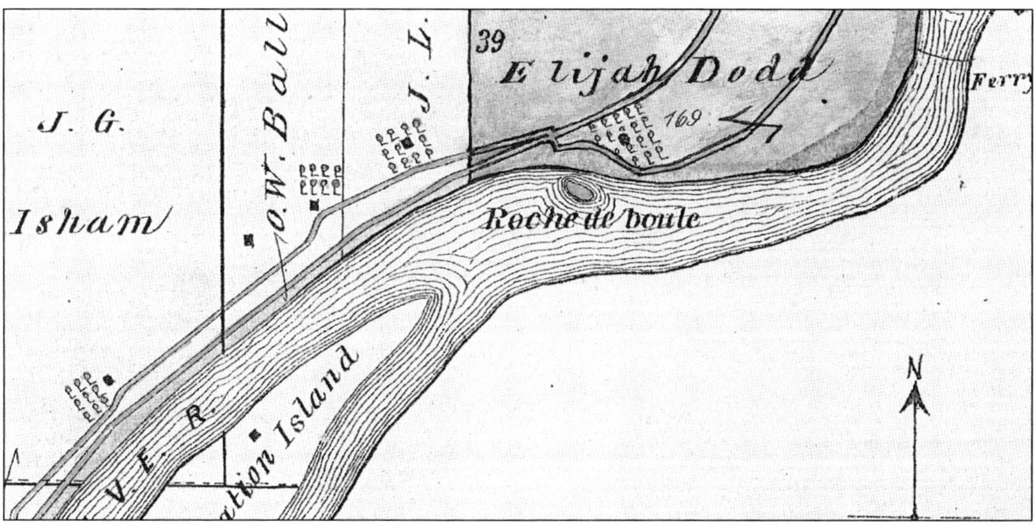

"Roche de Boule" is prominently marked on this map of Waterville in an 1875 Lucas County atlas. Elijah Dodd, the county's sheriff, owned a premium farm that overlooked the rock island. Note the ferry service operated by Dodd.

Waterville's Roche de Boeuf Festival has grown into one of the Maumee Valley's most popular community events. In 1996, artist Dorothy Yeack incorporated historical icons into the festival's logo. (Courtesy of *The Blade*, Toledo.)

This "Boeuf" (bison or buffalo) has become something of a mascot for Waterville. It has taken up permanent residency in front of Smedlap's Smithy Restaurant. (Courtesy of *The Blade*, Toledo.)

The Fort Meigs Cushing Company helped celebrate the 1984 Roche de Beouf Day with "a blast." (Courtesy of *The Blade*, Toledo.)

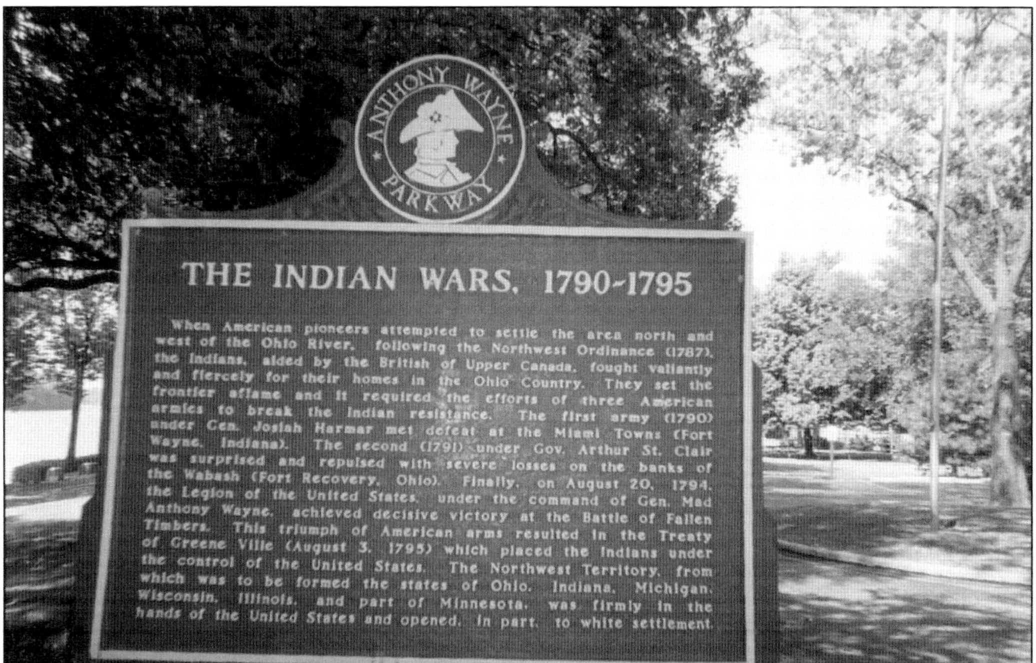

The Anthony Wayne Parkway erected this plaque at Farnsworth Park, upriver from Roche de Bout, in the 1950s.

Parkway plaques and other "Wayne Country" markers were highlighted in this c. 1955 tour guide. Per the publication's introduction:

In 1947, the Ohio General Assembly erected the Anthony Wayne Parkway Board to establish a memorial to Gen. Wayne and the heroes of the Indian Wars. In the 23 counties through which the campaigns were fought, a unified system of shrines and parks was developed. . . . Modern highways which closely follow the wilderness trails cut by Generals Harmar, St. Clair, and Wayne are marked as the Anthony Wayne Parkway. They guide the traveler to all of the old fort and battle sites, to beautiful parks, and to many other points of interest along the way—in the ANTHONY WAYNE COUNTRY.

A turn-of-the-century riverscape described as the Fallen Timbers Battlefield. Dr. G. Michael Pratt's dogged archival research and follow-up archaeological analysis have pointed to the probability that most of the conflict took place in the wet wood highland, not the lowland seen in this vista. (Courtesy of the Local History & Genealogy Department, Toledo-Lucas County Public Library.)

Four

FALLEN TIMBERS

The morning of August 20, 1794, began with a rumble of thunder and a rain shower. Wayne's men, who had slept with their firearms, had to reload and were late in breaking camp. Second-in-command Brigadier General James Wilkinson and his "cabal" questioned leaving an incomplete fortification and moving the army into a probable ambush.

The Legion reached the "island in the prairie," Presque Isle (French for peninsula). Below this prospect was arrayed a mile-long defensive line of an estimated force of more than one thousand Indians, as well as Queen's Rangers and Detroit militia disguised as Indians. Farther downriver were the log buildings of Alexander McKee's Indian Department post, McCormick's plantation, and the British Fort Miami. Between the garrison and Maumee Bay were three native villages swelling with refugees.

General Wayne himself described the army's advance, and what became briefly retreat, in a dispatch to Secretary of War Henry Knox. He reported that five miles out of Fort Deposit the mounted volunteers bore the first brunt of battle, receiving "so severe a fire from the enemy, who were secreted in the wood and high grass, as to compel them to retreat."

The Legion quickly responded and stiffened, snatching victory from the jaws of defeat, forming two lines "principally in a close thick wood . . . the ground being covered with old fallen timber, probably occasioned by a tornado." The front line was ordered to advance and "charge with trailed arms, and rouse the Indians from their coverts at the point of bayonet." A coordinated cavalry attack turned the Confederacy's flank, and the Battle of Fallen Timbers became the Route at the Rapids. Wrote the exultant "Mad Anthony," "[The] horde of savages, with their allies, abandoned themselves to flight, and dispersed with terror and dismay, leaving our victorious army in full and quiet possession of the field of battle."

Another eyewitness countered that the Indians had made "quite a show of fighting." Later historians were to express their admiration for the warriors and their decision to stand and fight for their families, their homelands, and their traditional ways of life.

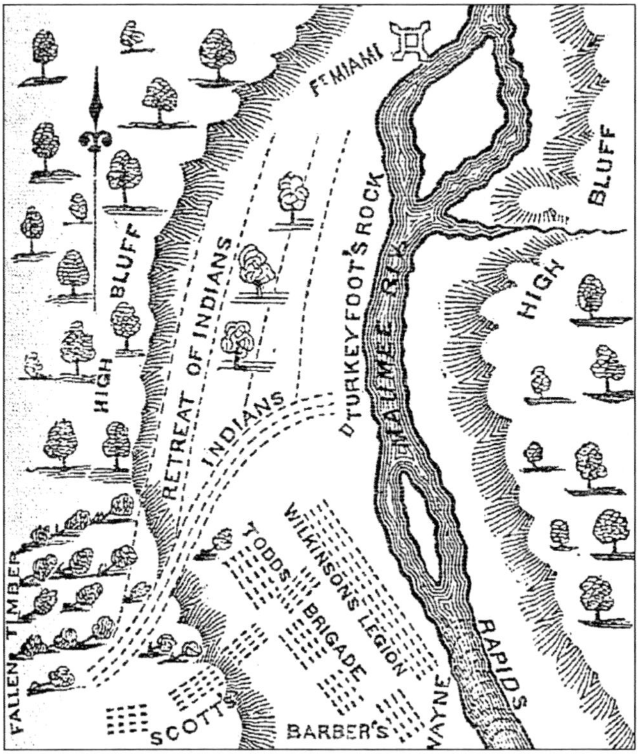

This 19th century conception of the battle was significantly altered by Dr. Pratt's discoveries.

An early 20th century snapshot with the inscription "Battle Ground of Fallen Timbers—August 28 [sic], 1794." The view is from the river, looking north. (Courtesy of the Local History and Genealogy Department, Toledo-Lucas County Public Library.)

(*above*) Tradition has it that two days before the Legion's encampment on Roche de Bout, representatives of the Shawnee, Ottawa, Miami, Cherokee, Chippewa, Wyandot, Huron, Delaware, Mingo, Pottawatomie, Sauk, Fox—among other Indian nations—convened at the rock island. Word of Wayne's juggernaut, rolling down the valley, had divided the ranks into advocates for submission and agitators for resistance. Little Turtle's call for acquiescence was more than countered by the Ottawa Egushawa's rousing appeal and warning to the Confederacy that it devolved upon those gathered to defend the council fires and graves of their ancestors. Thus, approximately one thousand Indians in common cause but diverse in geography and culture stood their ground. They would make their stand in a nature-made fort downstream, in a woods recently wracked by a windstorm.

(*left*) The Indian ambush line extended for nearly a mile, at an oblique angle to the river, on high ground. Approximately sixty of the Queen's Rangers and other Canadian militia formed the right flank. Several anecdotes have warriors rising from their cover with a bloodcurdling war-whoop as a signal for a mass enfilade.

"Opening of the Battle of Fallen Timbers" enhances Dr. Downes' *The Conquest.* The author affirmed, "It was horse that won the battle of Fallen Timbers; horses that dragged the heavy wagons from post to post through the woods and swamps between Cincinnati and Fort Deposit; horses which at 11 o'clock on the morning of August 20 suddenly reared as musket shots rang out from behind the brush and fallen tree trunks."

Dr. Downes described this scene, limned by art students at Scott High School in Toledo, by stating, "The infantry quickened its pace, the Indians were soon fleeing pell-mell from the battlefield."

Detail of a Presidential campaign poster for William Henry Harrison entitled "Harrison at Wayne's Victory." This vignette glorifies "Old Tip's" dash and daring at Fallen Timbers.

Another heroic battle scene involving the President-to-be. This plate is from a mid-19th century biography.

Frederick Kemmelmeyer's 1794 oil painting celebrating the victory of Wayne and his Legion at the Foot of the Rapids. Although the helmets of the horsemen are quite accurate, the mountains in the background are a far cry from Presque Isle hillock. (Courtesy of the Winterthur Museum.)

"Wayne's Defeat of the Indians," prepared for Benjamin Lossing's *A History of the United States* in 1860, correctly evoked the terrain of a wet wood but incorrectly had the Legion dressed in uniforms of the Revolutionary era.

"The Charge of the Dragoons" by Rufus Fairchild Zogbaum, enhanced an 1896 *Harper's New Monthly Magazine* feature story written by the Rough Rider-in-the-making, Theodore Roosevelt.

"The Battle of Fallen Timbers" graced several late 19th and early 20th century history books, including *The Story of the Greatest Nation*. The atmospheric play of shadow and light are evocative of the engravings of Frenchman Gustave Doré.

I like to recall 'the scenes of my childhood'
Where with boyish abandon and careless of care,
I swam in the river and wandered the wildwood
And believed the wild legends that they told me there.
Where the rippling water makes a soft rhyming
As it flows o'er the rapids of a long summer day,
And the wings of the fish birds with it keep timing
As they scan the bright waves in search of their prey.
At many a gem by nature's enchantment made perfect
I've gazed in mountain and glen;
That spot is a reflex of some part of heaven
And recalls and recalls me, again and again.
But when the dark storm binds low at midnight
The dread sounds are heard again and again.
'Tis the groans of the dying, the fall of the slain
The doom of the red man by Anthony Wayne.
When the tempest at midnight breaks o'er the valley
Then each to his home will quickly repair,
For the shrieks of the savage are heard on the rapids,
Wild shrieks of the Indian, mad yells of despair.
Then phantoms are seen, ghosts of the savage
From their death-dealing foe they flee as for life.
Then is heard the dull crash of the death-dealing sabre
And the rivet runs red from the unequal strife.
Then far o'er Presque Isle the wild sounds are wafted,
Echoed, re-echoed by hillside and dell;
Dread horror reigns, on mad nature engrafted
And earth is incarnate with mockings of hell.
And thus it has been since the day of the battle
When all of the tribe on the river were slain,
And thus it will be 'til the night of creation
While the hills and the rapids and rivers remain.

Topeka, Kansas January 2, 1892 Eugene N. Gunn

According to a former Waterville resident, the Battle of Fallen Timbers was still being waged by phantom combatants nearly a century after the Legion first clashed with the Confederacy.

Ein Kampf mit Indianern (A Fight with Indians) graces the pages of *Die Blockhutte in Maumeethale*. Authored by L.W. Grapp and published in Reading, Pennsylvania, 1894, the historical novel highlights both the Battle of Fallen Timbers and Dudley's Defeat. This generic print may represent either clash—or both. (Courtesy of the Canaday Center, Carlson Library, University of Toledo.)

The Italian artist Ettore Caser completed this mural for a People's Savings Bank of Toledo in 1930. (Courtesy of the Local History & Genealogy Department, Toledo-Lucas County Public Library.)

An aerial photographic view of the landscape that provided the setting for Caser's composition. It is the present location of the Wayne Monument and Battlefield Park. Archaeologist Dr. G. Michael Pratt has documented that the "fallen timbers" were located closer to Monclova, some distance from the Maumee River. (Courtesy of *The Blade*, Toledo.)

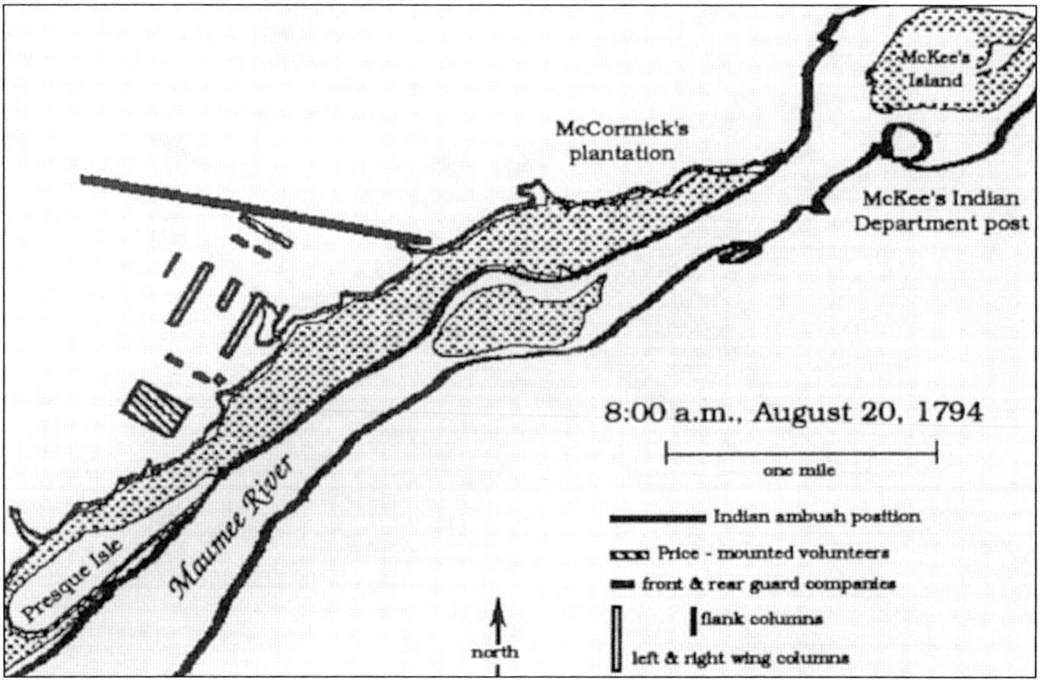

According to Dr. G. Michael Pratt, the battle—perhaps more correctly deemed a fight—lasted less than two hours, covered an area between two to four miles, and involved more than 3,000 individuals. Traditional accounts have the conflict ending at the barred gates of Fort Miamis, where the vanquished Indians were turned away by the British garrison. (Courtesy of Dr. Pratt.)

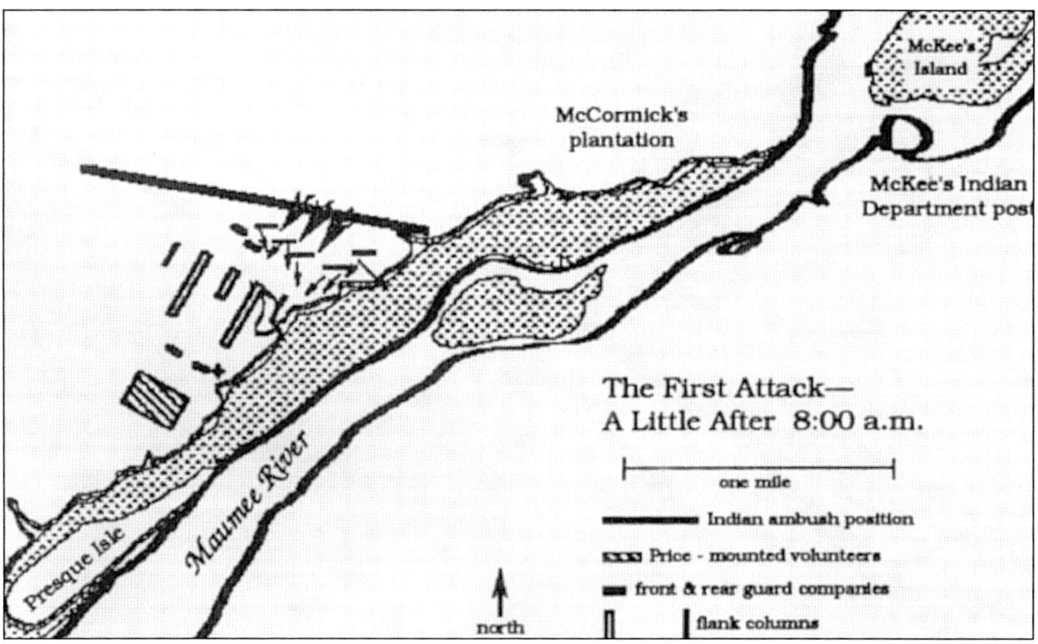

Pratt's second figure shows the initial surprise and success of the Confederacy ambush. Had Harmar or St. Clair and not Wayne been in command, the results may well have been disastrous for the Federal troops. (Courtesy of Dr. Pratt.)

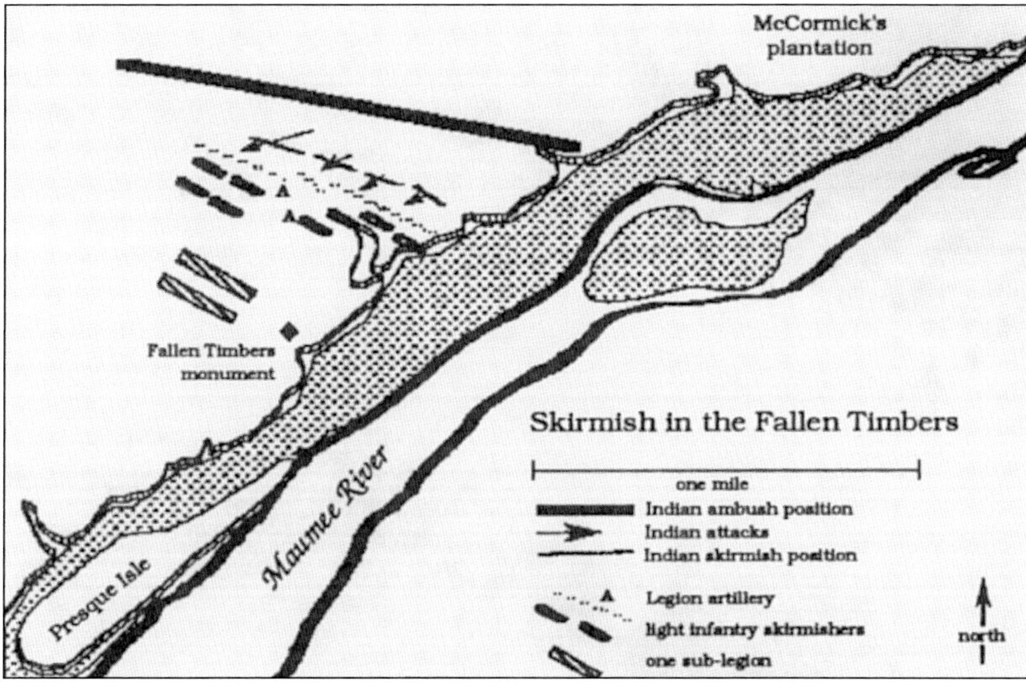

"The Skirmish in the Fallen Timbers" illustrates the fact that light infantry did rally after the opening volley and maintain their lines. (Courtesy of Dr. Pratt.)

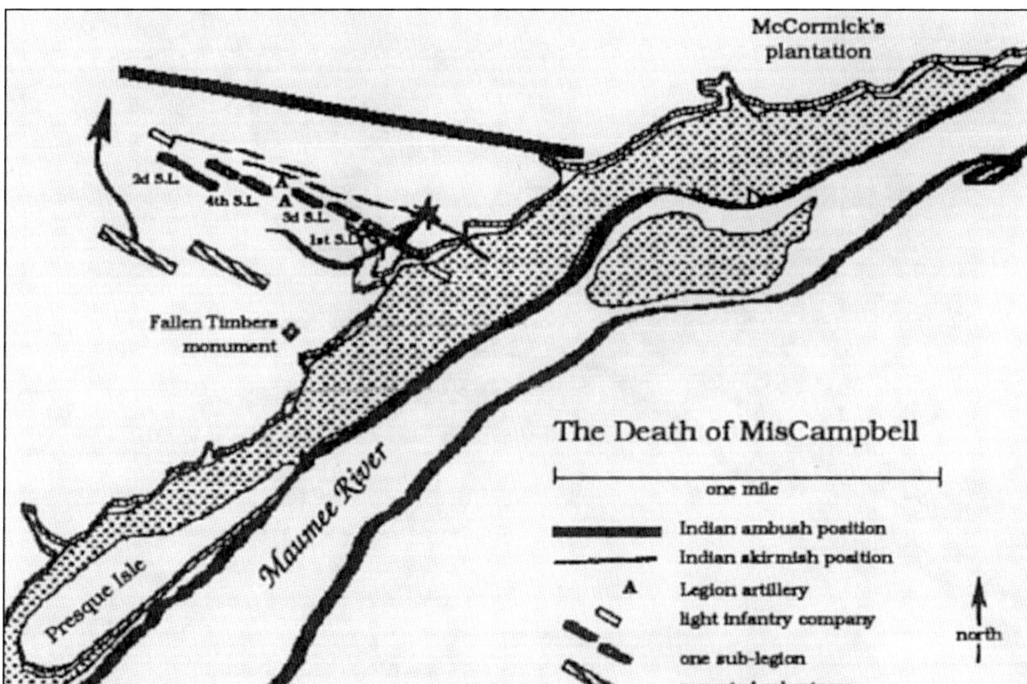

Captain Robert MisCampbell, commander of the dragoons, was slowed by the tangled trunks and branches. Comrade James Wilkinson recorded that "poor Mis Camble" [sic] had "mixed with (the enemy) and was killed with several of his men." (Courtesy of Dr. Pratt.)

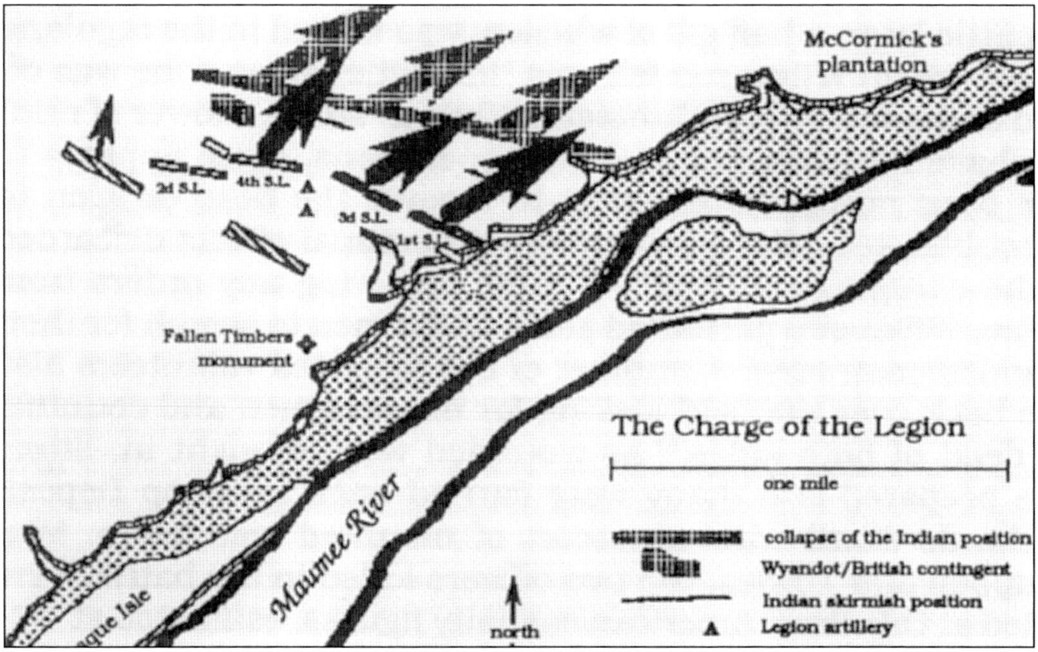

"The Charge of the Legion" was the subject of many heroic engravings and paintings seen in previous pages. (Courtesy of Dr. Pratt.)

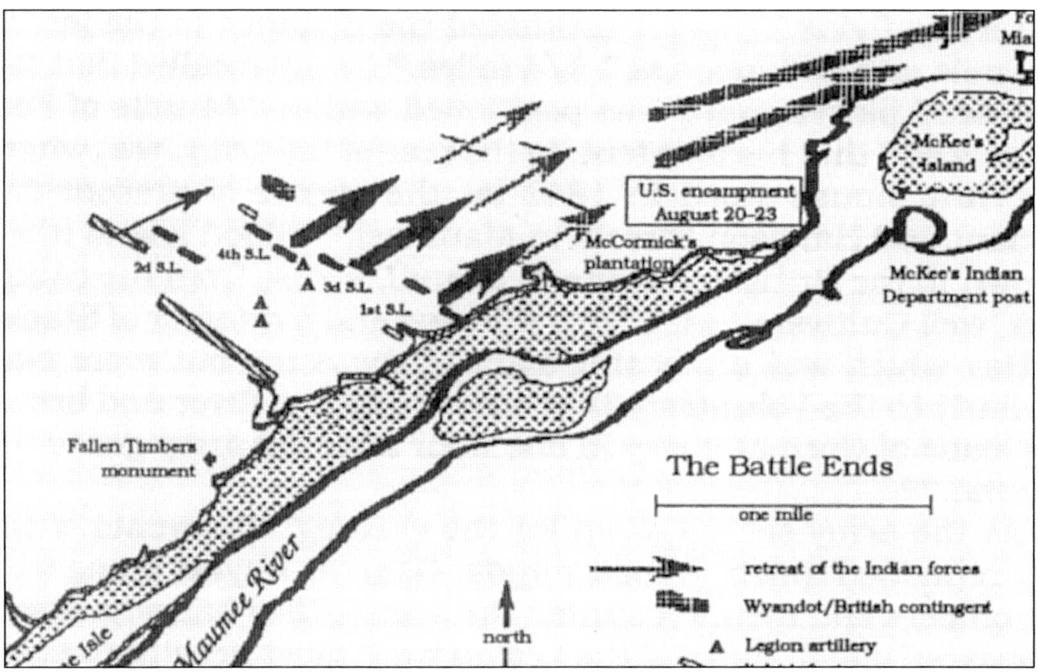

Dr. Pratt did agree with accounts that, for all intents and purposes, the conflict ended at the barred gates of Fort Miamis, where the vanquished Indians were turned away by the British. Concluded the archaeologist, "The failure of the British at Fort Miamis to take any kind of action against Wayne during the battle—or to protect their own Indian post and supplies in the aftermath—presented a clear message to the Indians that they were on their own." (Courtesy of Dr. Pratt.)

Dr. Pratt shows off two uniform buttons found in 1995 at the battle site near the State Route 24/Interstate 475 interchange. Additional artifacts recovered during metal detecting are in the tackle box. (Courtesy of *The Blade*, Toledo.)

General David Palmer, author of a 1794 retrospective, talks archaeology with William Block, Jr., co-president and publisher of *The Blade*; Jack Jaqua, battlefield preservation coordinator; and Dr. Pratt. (Courtesy of *The Blade*, Toledo.)

Maumee Mayor Kent C. Gardam and his executive officer Tom Crothers examine archaeological findings, June 1995. These and other artifacts helped Pratt piece together the troop movements seen in his "time-lapse maps." (Courtesy of *The Blade*, Toledo.)

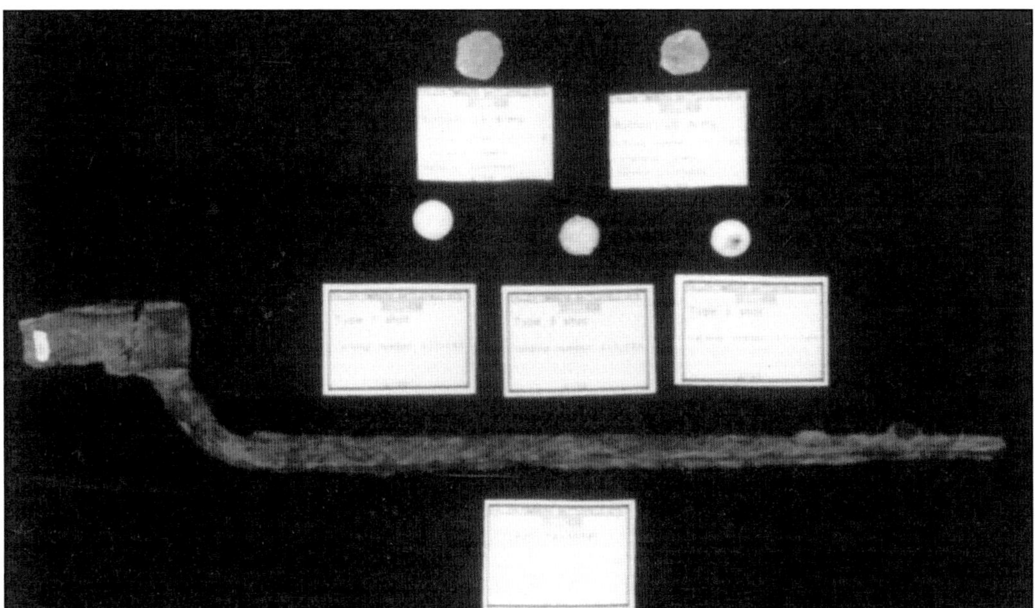

Among the items recovered from the 1995 archaeological project were a socket bayonet and musket balls. (Courtesy of *The Blade*, Toledo.)

The two musket balls at left and center show teeth marks where the bullet has been used, possibly during surgery. The one on the right bears a hole indicating that it was jammed and drawn out. (Courtesy of *The Blade*, Toledo.)

Affiliate Unit

The Battle of Fallen Timbers

NEWSLETTER

70 YEARS!

METROPARKS
TOLEDO AREA

May, 2001 — Volumn 1, No 1

Communicating News of the Fallen Timbers Battlefield National Historic Site

Public Field Archaeology Slated

More Artifacts Found on Battlefield

Archaeological research on the battlefield is going well, if not quite according to plan.

The effort to gather baseline archaeological information has weathered an early and unusually snowy winter and an inclement spring, but there's been progress. Five of eight established units have been included in the work. The remaining three units and a section of the woods slated for study remain too wet for archaelological investigation.

In early December Metroparks crews were able to mow down the corn stubble left by last year's farming operation. The day they finished heavy snowfall moved into the area and kept the battlefield locked in snow for several months.

In early April Dr. G. Michael Pratt supervised Historic Archaeology Research, Inc., in its efforts to establish a permanent grid for future archaeological research and to establish survey areas at the location where buttons were found in the 1995 survey. They worked one day when torrential rains deluged the battlefield and left it an unworkable quagmire.

A second visit April 27–29 was more successful, with more than 85 additional battle artifacts recovered including 29 uniform buttons, musket and rifle balls, and buckshot.

The spring survey set the stage for the Public Field Archaeology Project which begins June 9 and continues through June 24.

Rich Green operates electronic imaging equipment as part of the battlefield archaeology survey.

more photos on page 4

Dr. Pratt's initial archaeological investigation led to a second intensive "expedition" in 2000–2001. The battle artifacts recovered—among them the head of a belt axe or tomahawk and the vestiges of a musket—provided historians with a better understanding of equipment and deployment. (Courtesy of Metroparks of the Toledo Area.)

Fallen Timbers Committee Meets With National Park Service

Readying the Fallen Timbers Battlefield and Fort Miamis National Historic Site for public use as an affiliated unit of the National Park Service will be an intense but rewarding effort that could take five to ten years, members of the Fallen Timbers Advisory Commission learned last November.

The Commission, which is composed of representatives from the diverse groups and organizations who worked together to acquire the Battlefield, met with representatives of the National Park Service (NPS) for an introduction to what will happen in the months ahead.

"Our goal will be to achieve a General Management Plan for the site in one and one-half to two years," Sandra Washington, chief planner for NPS Midwest Region, told the group. "It will be five to ten years to bricks and mortar. Permanent facilities can't be built until planning is complete and all cultural and environmental impacts are measured.

"The process can be sped up with the use of local funding," she added.

But NPS officials supported suggestions that public programming can be started and some temporary site improvements might be possible much sooner.

Governor Bob Taft pauses with Joyce Mahaney (left), founder of the American Indian Intertribal Association, and Barbara Hunt at the Fallen Timbers Monument where the Governor presented Ohio's check for $2.5 million to help purchase the battlefield.

Metroparks currently owns 66.8 acres of the 185-acre battlefield, and has a commitment to purchase the remaining acreage by July 31, 2001.

NPS is expected to have $100,000 in the next fiscal year to initiate planning, with another $100,000 expected the following year.

Planning Process Could Start Soon

Metroparks officials have been informed that the National Park Service does not have a staff person available to act as a planning facilitator and that an outside consultant will be hired to fill that role. Sandra Washington, chief planner for NPS Midwest Region headquartered in Omaha, Nebraska, said that someone from her planning staff would be assigned to oversee and coordinate the process.

The consultant could be hired in May and the process could begin within a few weeks of that commitment.

According to the May 2001 (premiere edition) of *The Battle of Fallen Timbers Newsletter*, "Readying the Fallen Timbers Battlefield and Fort Miamis National Historic Site for public use as an affiliated unit of the National Park Service will be an intense but rewarding effort that could take five to ten years." (Courtesy of Metroparks of the Toledo Area.)

A special resources study laid the groundwork for the NPS affiliation. The document incorporated the results of the 1995 archaeological project. (Courtesy of Metroparks of the Toledo Area.)

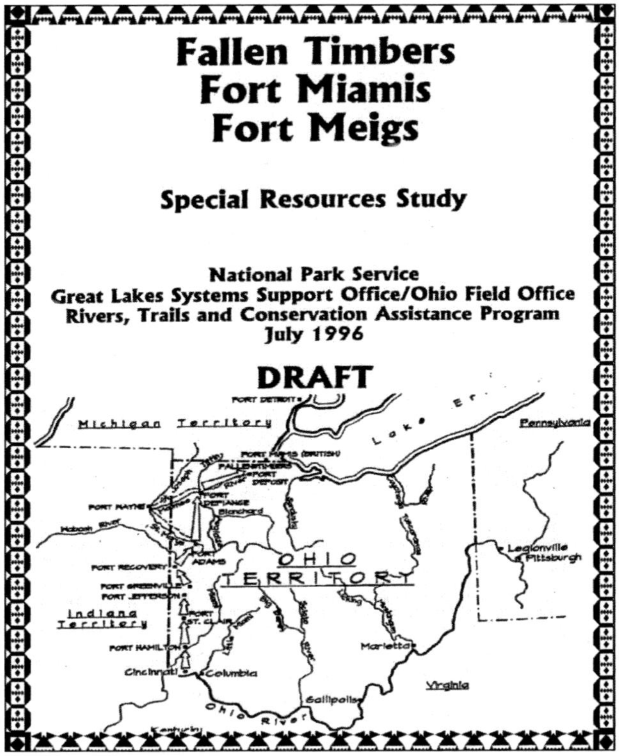
Fallen Timbers
Fort Miamis
Fort Meigs

Special Resources Study

National Park Service
Great Lakes Systems Support Office/Ohio Field Office
Rivers, Trails and Conservation Assistance Program
July 1996

DRAFT

106th Congress

An Act

Dec. 9, 1999
[S. 548]

To establish the Fallen Timbers Battlefield and Fort Miamis National Historical Site in the State of Ohio.

Be it enacted by the Senate and House of Representatives of the United States of America in Congress assembled,

Fallen Timbers Battlefield and Fort Miamis National Historic Site Act of 1999. 16 USC 461 note.

SECTION 1. SHORT TITLE.

This Act may be cited as the "Fallen Timbers Battlefield and Fort Miamis National Historic Site Act of 1999".

SEC. 2. DEFINITIONS.

As used in this Act:

(1) The term "historic site" means the Fallen Timbers Battlefield and Monument and Fort Miamis National Historic Site established by section 4 of this Act.

(2) The term "management plan" means the general management plan developed pursuant to section 5(d).

(3) The term "Secretary" means the Secretary of the Interior.

(4) The term "management entity" means the Metropolitan Park District of the Toledo Area.

(5) The term "technical assistance" means any guidance, advice, or other aid, other than financial assistance, provided by the Secretary.

The new century began with two new National Historical Sites, the Fallen Timbers Battlefield and Fort Miamis.

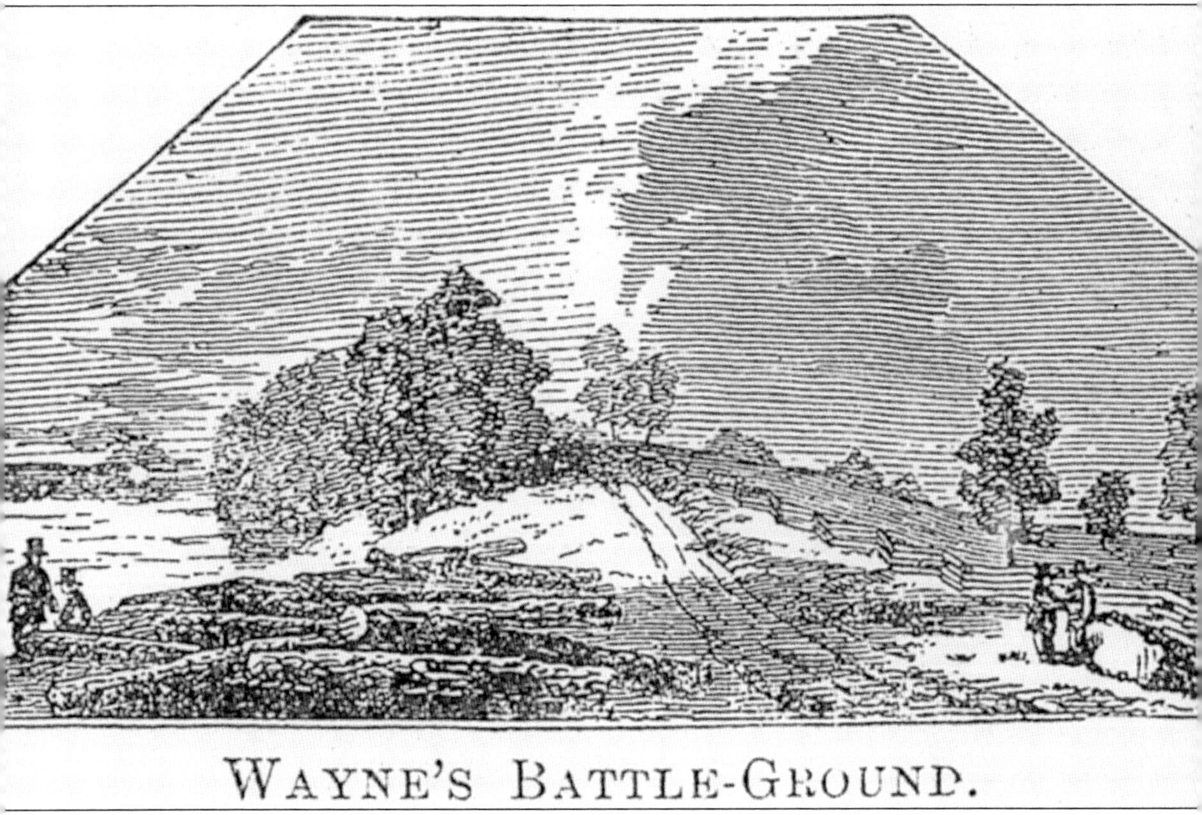

Two wayfarers pause at Turkey Foot Rock in "Wayne's Battle-Ground," an engraving prepared for *Historical Collections of Ohio* (1888). Author-illustrator Henry Howe recorded, "The early settlers and travelers through the Maumee Valley usually found small pieces of tobacco deposited on this rock, which had been placed there by Indians as devotional acts by way of sacrifice, to appease the indignant spirit of the departed hero."

Five

Turkey Foot Rock and the Monument

General Wayne reported to Knox, "The woods were stewed for a considerable distance with the dead bodies of Indians and their white Auxiliaries." Adding to the carnage were the seven score of dead and wounded Legionnaires and militiamen left in the wake of the assault. Finally bowing to the impassioned appeals of his subordinates, the cautious, if not callous, Wayne authorized recovery and burial. The native and Canadian remains were likely attended by the Confederacy and the British upon the Legions' withdrawal up the valley.

Although early 19th-century visitors to the Foot of the Rapids occasioned upon relics and other grisly remnants (including the entwined skeletons of a Legionnaire and an Indian, forever locked in mortal combat!) to remind them of the great Battle of Fallen Timbers, traces of the war-torn battlefield were rapidly reclaimed by nature. As early as the 1830s, the editor of the weekly newspaper, *The Maumee Express*, was moved to compose a "Lest We Forget" letter to his readers. He affirmed that theirs was among the most historic and hallowed sites in the entire United States, and implored his fellow patriotic citizens to make pilgrimages to Wayne's Battle Ground. Two landmarks in particular, one traditional and one neoclassical, were to help entice those pilgrims in decades to come. Turkey Foot Rock and the Wayne Monument/Fallen Timbers Memorial, if they do not mark the precise place of an epic struggle, do pay apt tribute to the heroes of an epic victory—and an epic defeat.

Andrew Coffinberry was born in Virginia, but spent most of his life practicing law in Perrysburg. He qualifies as one of the Maumee Valley's most colorful, if not slightly eccentric, pioneers. His manner of dress—according to a contemporary, "colonial style excepting the short knee breeches"—earned him the title "Count."

"Count" Coffinberry penned an epic of the Battle of Fallen Timbers in 1842. His depiction of Ottawa Chief Turkey Foot is comparable to any Homeric hero.

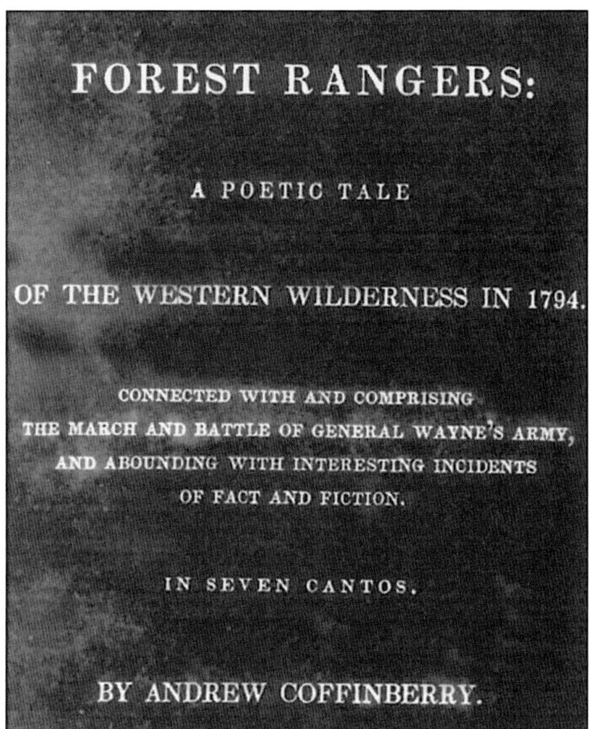

FOREST RANGERS:

A POETIC TALE

OF THE WESTERN WILDERNESS IN 1794.

CONNECTED WITH AND COMPRISING
THE MARCH AND BATTLE OF GENERAL WAYNE'S ARMY,
AND ABOUNDING WITH INTERESTING INCIDENTS
OF FACT AND FICTION.

IN SEVEN CANTOS.

BY ANDREW COFFINBERRY.

. . . . at the Foot of red Presque Isle
Brave Me-sa-sa was warring still
He stood upon a large rough stone
Still dealing blows alone
But bleeding fast; glazed were his eyes
And feeble grew his battle cries
Too frail his arms, too dim his sight
To wield or aim his ax aright
As still more frail and faint he grew
His body on the rock he threw
As coursed his blood along the ground
In feeble, low and hollow sound
Mingled with frantic peals and strong
The dying chief poured forth (a) song.

This comical interpretation of the demise of Chief Turkey Foot was drawn by R.M. Brinkerhoff for *Men of Toledo and Their Neighbors* (*The Blade*, Toledo, c. 1900).

Death of Turkey Foot
At Battle of Fallen Timbers

In the early 20th century, the boulder was "enhanced" with interpretive signage.

A surreal scene at Presque Isle, courtesy of the Berkshire Life Insurance Company of Pittsfield, Massachusetts. Chief Turkey Foot lies prostrate in the shadow of his boulder while "Mad Anthony" and a "caballero" accept a peace offering from a Plains Indian-styled supplicant.

Both sign and postcards did much to embroider the already extravagant saga of *Me-sa-sa*: "Chief Turkey Foot being totally wounded crawled to this rock and tomahawked three turkey's feet on this rock, so identification could be made."

"Turkey-Foot's Rock" was engraved for *The Pictorial Field-Book of the War of 1812* (Harper & Brothers, 1896). Wrote *Field-Book* author Benson Lossing:

> *Among the brave warriors in the battle who were the last to flee before Wayne's Legion, was Me-sa-sa, or Turkey-Foot, an Ottawa chief, who lived on Blanchard's Fork of the Au Glaize River. He was greatly beloved by his people. His courage was conspicuous. When he found the line of dusky warriors giving way at the foot of Presque Isle Hill, he leaped upon a small boulder, and by his voice and gesture endeavored to make them stand firm. He almost immediately fell, pierced by a musket ball, and expired by the side of the rock. Long years afterward, when any of his tribe passed along the Maumee trail, they would stop at that rock, and linger a long time with manifestations of sorrow.*

Turkey Foot Rock was easily accessible to pilgrim and vandal alike. Graffiti "artists" added inscriptions, and it became difficult, if not impossible, to differentiate the "Me-sa-san" from the malicious.

In anticipation of the Ohio Centennial in 1903, some ardent residents of Toledo claimed Turkey Foot Rock as their prize and removed it to the Lucas County seat. The boulder's return merited an elaborate—to quote Maumee historian John Gunckel—"reception and jollification" by the citizens of Maumee.

The rock was returned to its River Road roost, and a perimeter of post and chains was installed to deter the ill-intended. (Courtesy of *The Blade*, Toledo.)

The authenticity of Turkey Foot Rock had been challenged by scholars for decades. In 1965, one skeptic proposed that the landmark was an imposter, and that the "Real McCoy" was actually embedded in a derelict foundation across the road. Lucas County sanitary engineer Raymond Hall and William Noyes, with University of Toledo history professor Randolph Downes (right), investigated. (Courtesy of *The Blade*, Toledo.)

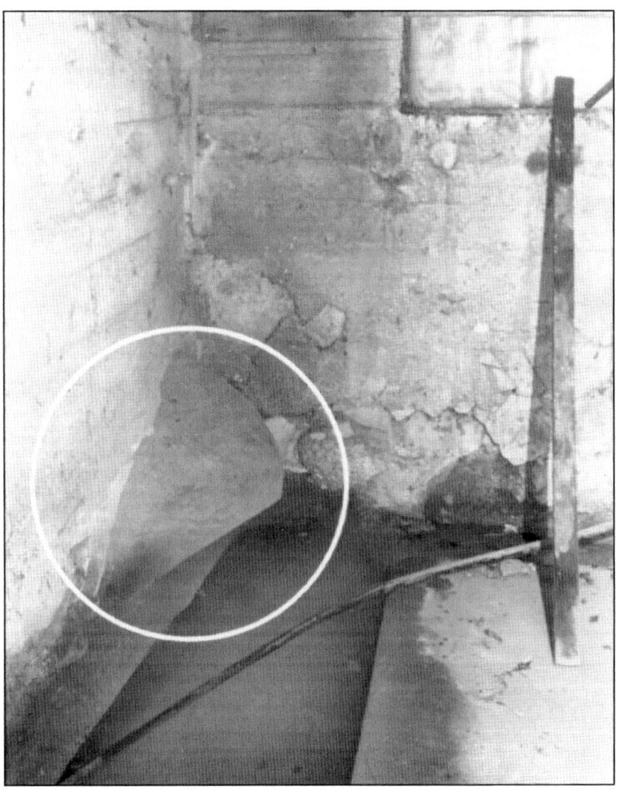

The investigators found a partially exposed boulder in proximity to a sulfur spring complete with an electric pump. (Courtesy of *The Blade*, Toledo.)

The University of Toledo's dean of pharmacy (with hat) and instructor Marshall Becker joined Downes in a thorough examination of the rock. They detected glacial grooves, but no turkey's feet or other petroglyphs. (Courtesy of *The Blade*, Toledo.)

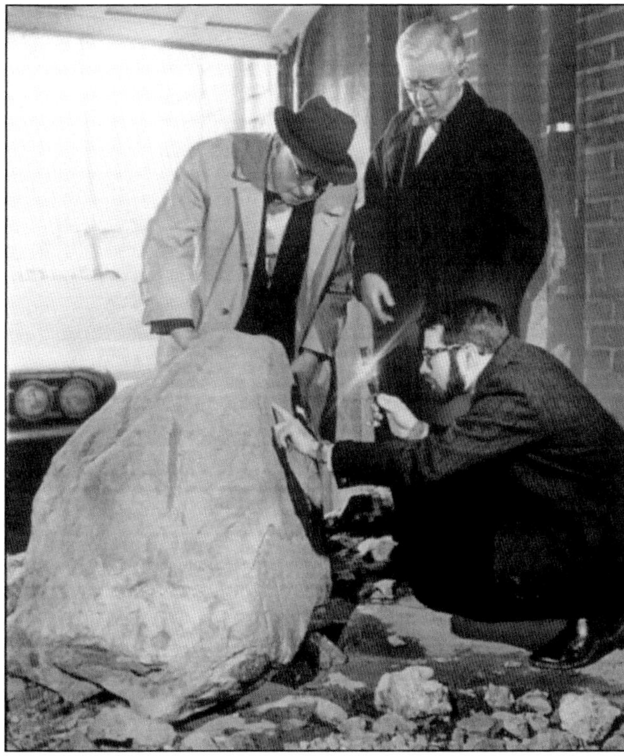

The lower Maumee Valley is littered with "erratic" glacial boulders, all of them potential candidates for the "true" Turkey Foot Rock.

The bluffs above the floodplain—and Turkey Foot Rock—provided what was thought to be the ideal location for a state memorial to Wayne and his Legion.

Bruce Wilder Saville was commissioned to sculpt the monument. This plaster prototype differs from the final sculpture in a number of details; compare this photograph with the finished monument seen on the following pages.

Dignitaries, members of the press, and hundreds of northwest Ohio residents attend the unveiling and dedication of the General Wayne Monument, September 14, 1929. (Courtesy of Jack Hiles.)

A panorama of the public parking on the floodplain below the monument, September 14, 1929. (Courtesy of Jack Hiles.)

Imogene Van Camp, a lineal descendant of William Sloane, a bugler in Wayne's Legion, pulled the cord that unveiled the monument. The cover of the 1929 unveiling and dedication program was embellished with art deco flourishes.

Bruce Wilder Saville was a graduate of The Ohio State University and a veteran of the First World War. His General Anthony Wayne Monument/Battle of Fallen Timbers Memorial was modeled in the heroic neoclassical style, and provided the basis for a commemorative postage stamp, one in a long line of "Two Cent Reds."

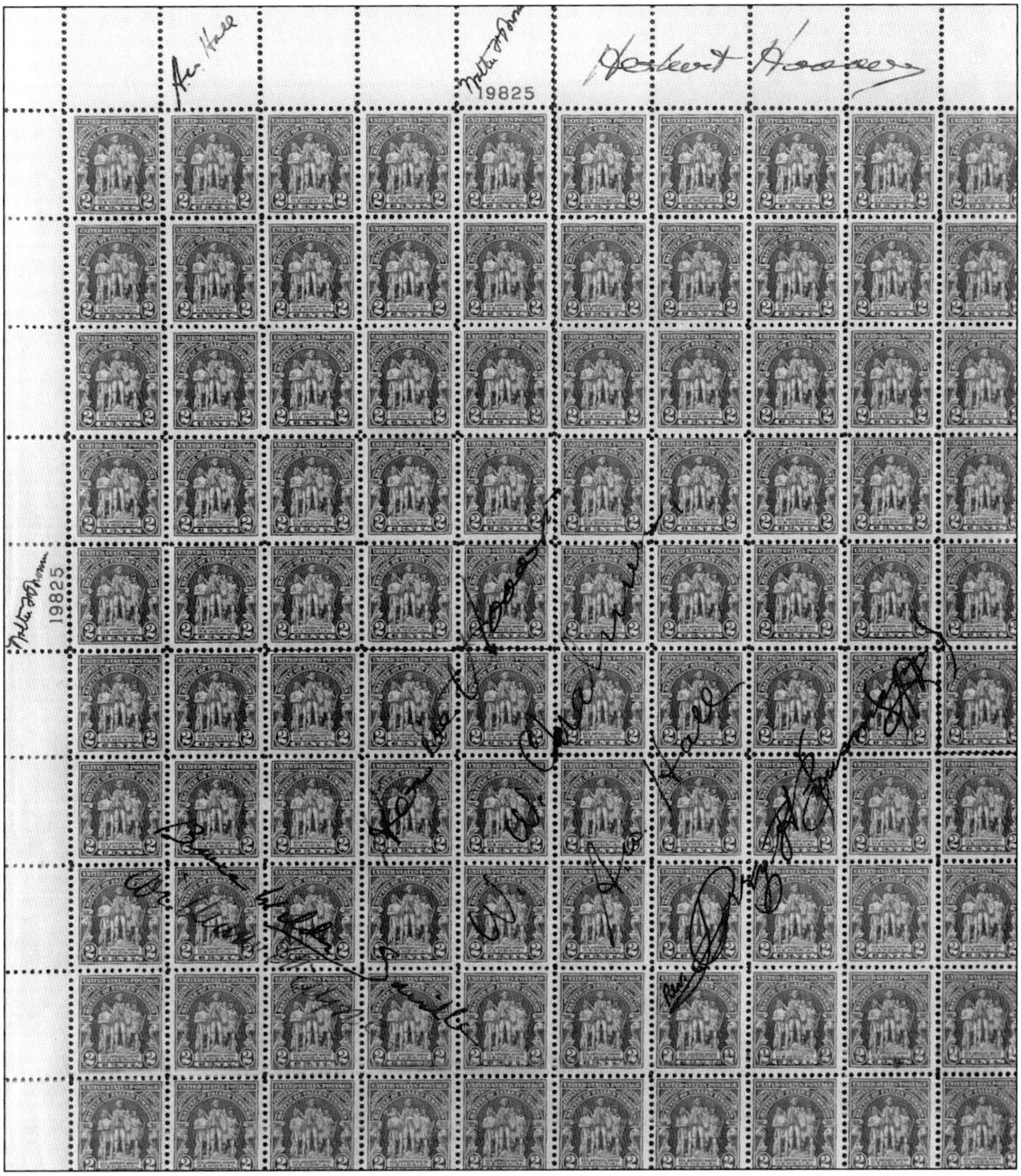

This unique sheet of Battle of Fallen Timbers postage stamps, the first off the printing press, was signed by President Herbert Hoover; Postmaster General Walter F. Brown (a Toledoan who was instrumental in facilitating the issuance of the commemorative); A.W. Hall, Chief of the Bureau of Engraving and Printing; U.S. Senator W.W. Chambers; Sculptor Bruce Wilder Saville; and the "father" of the stamp, the Reverend Perry H. Baumann. (Courtesy of the Local History & Genealogy Department, Toledo-Lucas County Public Library.)

FALLEN TIMBERS

A special two-cent postage stamp will be issued on September 14th as a memorial to General Anthony Wayne and to commemorate the 135th anniversary of the Battle of Fallen Timbers. This battle resulted in peace with the Indians in northwestern Ohio, evacuation of the last traces of British soldiery in this section and put the young American nation in position to expand westward.

The new stamp will first be placed on sale on September 14th in four cities in Ohio and one city in Pennsylvania.

FOR ONLY $1.00 we will send you first day covers of the new stamp from the five cities which will have it on the first day of sale. We will send you also an unused block of four of the new stamp, mailed to you from Washington on the first day of sale here.

FOR ONLY $2.75 we will send you a complete sheet of 100 stamps, mailed to you from Washington on the first day of sale here (Sept. 16). This sheet will be sent by air mail in an air mail envelope franked with copies of the Fallen Timbers stamp.

RUSH YOUR ORDERS

SCOTT 1930 STANDARD POSTAGE STAMP CATALOG. The new 1930 edition of the Scott catalog will be issued about the 28th of October. May we have your order for it? The price is $2.00 and we will send it postpaid to any part of the U. S. We will pay the postage with various commemorative stamps, including the scarce 2c and 5c Hawaii surcharges, the 2c Molly Pitcher, and other varieties to make up the necessary amount of postage. Please send cash with order.

C. E. NICKLES, 213 Seaton Pl., N. E., Washington, D. C.

"RUSH YOUR ORDERS" for first-day covers of the Fallen Timbers commemorative, urged C.E. Nickles of the nation's capital. This postcard was sent to the stamp dealer's clients in late August of 1929.

This multicolored postcard was especially prepared for the Fallen Timbers stamp's first day of issuance at Erie, Pennsylvania, the site of Wayne's death. It is prized as one of the rarest September 14, 1929, philatelic collectables.

THE ANTHONY WAYNE MEMORIAL JOINT LEGISLATIVE COMMITTEE
AT FALLEN TIMBERS

Left to right: Harold W. Carr, Raymond H. Burke, Roy H. Longenecker, Fred L. Adams, Guy D. Hawley, Fred L. Hoffman, Jr., Margaret A. Mahoney, Theodore M. Gray. Not present: Roy E. Harmony and Fred R. Seibert.

The movers and shakers of the Anthony Wayne Parkway gathered at the monument. This group portrait was taken as World War II drew to a close.

A 1936 snapshot of the monument reveals a flagpole (since removed) and circular driveway (since closed to vehicular traffic). (Courtesy of *The Blade*, Toledo.)

Another snapshot shows a "naked" hillside. The area has been allowed to go to its natural state and by the end of the century was covered with wildflowers, tall grasses, shrubs, and other growth. (Courtesy of *The Blade*, Toledo.)

In 1954, the memorial site literally became another fallen timbers battlefield. The public decried the state's removal of trees for a new access road to the sculpture. (Courtesy of *The Blade*, Toledo.)

The former access came off River Road. The new avenue, as this aerial photograph indicates, is easily accessible from the bustling Anthony Wayne Trail. (Courtesy of *The Blade*, Toledo.)

Perhaps one of the more artistic, indeed dramatic, views of the monument is depicted in this photograph taken for the travel section of a newspaper. (Courtesy of *The Blade*, Toledo.)

Turkey Foot Rock was moved from its River Road location to its present location near the base of the Wayne Monument in the mid-20th century. The plaque memorializing the American Indians lost in the battle was erected four decades later.

Interpretive markers were installed by the Ohio Historical Society in the 1970s. This panel features a svelte Revolutionary War-era likeness of General Wayne, a far cry from the portly and gout-ridden "Old Tony" of 1794.

An unusual winter view of monument and rock. (Courtesy of *The Blade*, Toledo.)

In 1984, the corroded, guano-ed monument received a much-needed conservation treatment. Here Anthony Zappone administers a pressure wash. (Courtesy of *The Blade*, Toledo.)

The reliefs at the base were all removed, cleaned, and replaced. Henry Lammie and Jack Middaugh provided the bronze settlers with tender loving care. (Courtesy of *The Blade*, Toledo.)

Upon the bicentennial of the Battle of Fallen Timbers, August 20, 1994, celebrants balanced the historical record by commissioning and dedicating a Native American memorial. Mike Faehle checked the plaque for scratches before it was set upright on its base. Courtesy of *The Blade*, Toledo.

The monument was unveiled in the midst of a late summer shower. (Courtesy of *The Blade*, Toledo.)

The bicentennial observance included an Indian powwow. (Courtesy of *The Blade*, Toledo.)

The 1994 festivities included living history vignettes. History gave way to hysteria when trail guide Bob Jackey was grabbed by Scouts Michael Soncrant (left) and Corey Eckel. (Courtesy of *The Blade*, Toledo.)

Dave Dysard (right) portrayed Blue Jacket , and Phil Skeldon, Little Turtle, in a scene from a Fallen Timbers "mellerdramer." (Courtesy of *The Blade*, Toledo.)

Six

Camp Foot of the Rapids

Early on in their explorations, Europeans recognized the commercial and militarily strategic importance of the Foot of the Rapids. It offered the link for navigation between the Maumee River and Lake Erie. The whitewater and placid estuary below teemed with sturgeon, walleye, bass, and other game fish. The arable lower Maumee Valley was exploited as acorn belt. Positioned between the virgin hardwood forests, oak openings, and marshy wasteland stretching to Detroit and an impenetrable Black Swamp, the region provided an oasis for a booming fur trade.

The British gained a toehold in the lower Detroit Country with the establishment of McKee's Indian Department post, and Lieutenant Governor Simcoe made a play for fortifying British claims—and openly defying American sovereignty—with the erection of Fort Miamis. That brazen, open defiance metamorphosed into rather passive resistance as Wayne progressed down the Maumee valley.

The North Bend, or Channel, as it came to be known by later inhabitants, was witness to not one, but two great showdowns between the British and the Americans. Along one two-mile stretch of the Maumee were situated two forts (Miamis and Meigs), Wayne's Camp Foot of the Rapids, Tecumseh's Crossing, the scene of Dudley's "Massacre," and several sites listed on the National Register of Historic Places, including a home built for the daughter of Captain Wells and the granddaughter of Little Turtle. Local historian John Gunckel avowed that Americans would be hard-pressed to find a comparable heartland of history.

The Legion had swept the field of battle, and "Mad Anthony" called a halt to the advance at the Foot of the Rapids. Wayne's admirers likened the campaign to his brilliant triumph at Stony Point during the American Revolution; his critics lambasted "Old Tony" for leaving behind the Legion wounded, as well as for exaggerating a "total victory" over the Confederacy.

The idyllic upriver of the vista of the Maumee Valley was blighted by the carnage in the wake of Fallen Timbers; reported Wayne, "The woods were strewed for a considerable distance with the dead bodies of Indians and their white auxiliaries." Decades after the battle, Maumee City sprouted up where the General established his Camp Foot of the Rapids.

One day after the Battle of Fallen Timbers, Lt. Boyer entered in his journal, "Camp Foot of the Rapids—21 August 1794. We are lying within half a mile of British Garrison." General Wayne elaborated:

We remained three days and nights on the banks of the Maumee, in front of the field of battle, during which time all the houses and corn-fields were consumed and destroyed for a considerable distance, both above and below Fort Miamis as well as within pistol-shot of the garrison, who were compelled to remain tacit spectators to this general devastation and conflagration.

GENERAL WAYNE'S DAILY ENCAMPMENT.

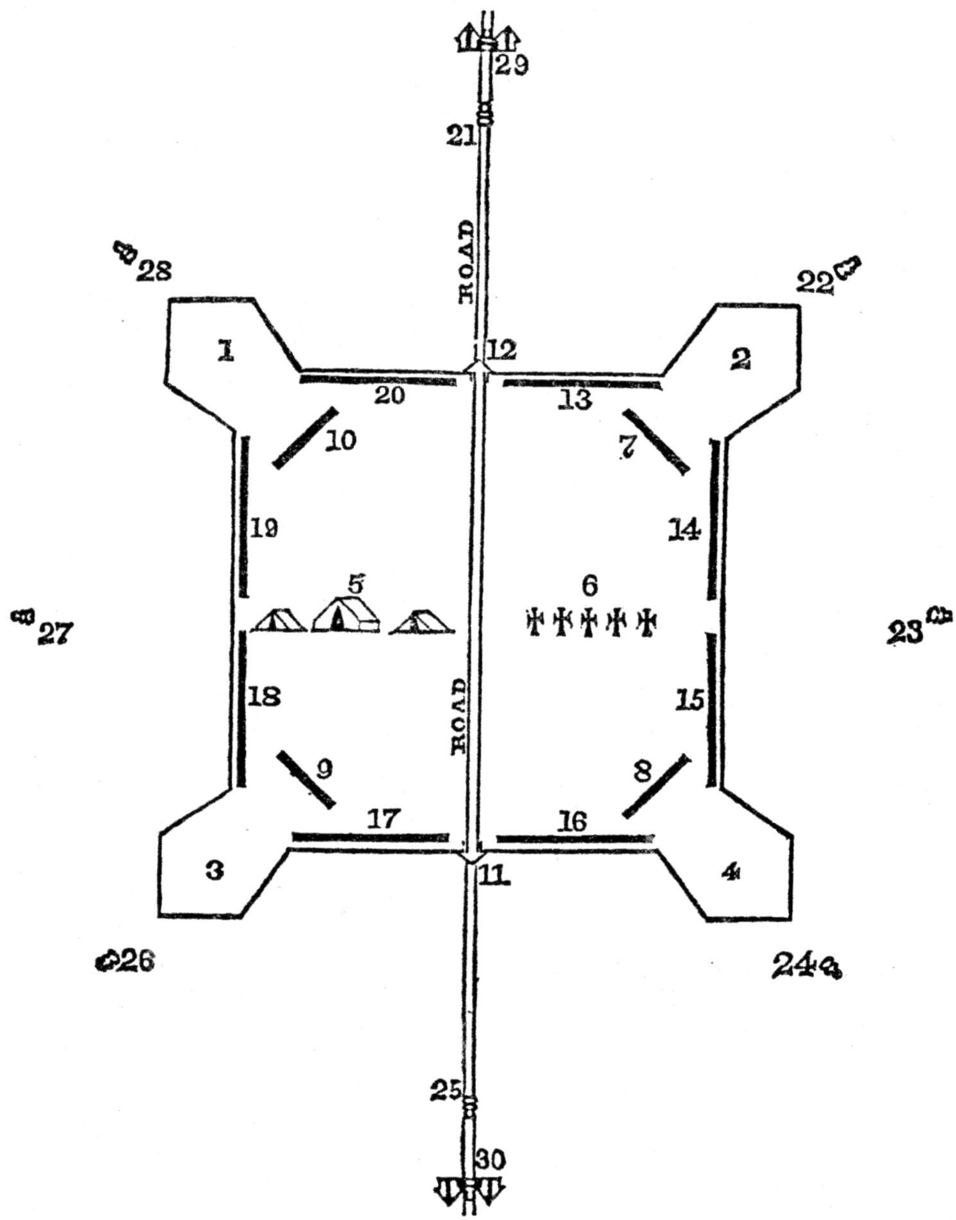

REFERENCE.

1. Lieutenant Massie's bastion.
2. Lieutenant Pope's bastion
3. Captain Porter's bastion.
4. Captain Ford's bastion.

11. Rear gateway.
12. Front gateway.
13 and 14. Third sub-legion.
15 and 16. First sub-legion.

Captain Daniel Brady recorded, "After the action which lasted about forty minutes, the army march'd & encamped in sight of the British garrison which is at the foot of the rapids—here we lay till August 23." The encampment more or less followed this configuration that was originally illustrated in *The American Pioneer* (1843).

This postcard view of Great Island (also known as Ewing, Pilliod, and Audubon Island), photographed *c.* 1910 from Perrysburg, reveals that hay was still being cultivated more than a century after the Legion had torched Alexander McKee's fields.

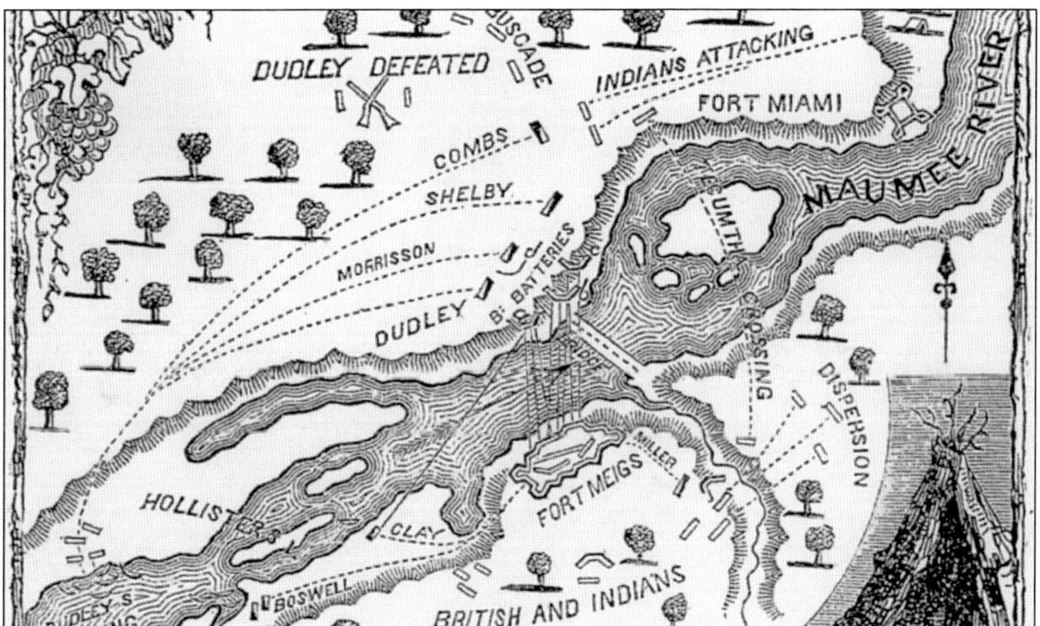

The upland between Camp Foot of the Rapids and Fort Miamis became the "slaughter pen" of "Dudley's Massacre" during the War of 1812. Colonel William Dudley and his zealous Kentucky detachment, after spiking British cannons, were overwhelmed by American Indian forces. A late 19th century map of the Foot of the Rapids traces the series of movements associated with Colonel Dudley's ill-fated offensive. According to this cartographer, Tecumseh (Tecumtha) intercepted his warriors and their captives on the present site of the Wolcott House Museum Complex.

This historical marker stands in front of the Maumee Public Library along River Road.

Tecumseh, upon reaching the scene of "Dudley's Massacre," is said to have burst out, "For shame, desist! It is a disgrace to kill a defenseless prisoner!" He told the British commander Henry Proctor, who had stood by and watched as the Kentuckians were maimed and killed, to "put on petticoats."

Mary Wells Wolcott, the daughter of Wayne's Captain of Spies and granddaughter of Little Turtle, made her home between the former sites of Camp Foot of the Rapids and Fort Miamis. Her father scouted this very bend of the river three decades before Mrs. Wolcott's arrival in Maumee.

Rilla Hull, the last of the Wells-Wolcott line to occupy the pioneer mansion on the Maumee, possessed three different silhouettes in the likeness of Captain Wells' daughters, one of which was Mary Wells Wolcott. Might this be Mrs. Wolcott?

Seven

Fort Miamis

The blood and smoke that transformed the civilization of North America are ingrained in the atmosphere and soil of the ancient site of the historic Fort Miami.
—The Blade, *September 14, 1940*

Early local historians confused Fort Miami with a French outpost built in the late 17th century. They went as far as to state that the alleged garrison was the "earliest settlement in Ohio by a good many years."

It was not until 1944 that the first in-depth research of the site was conducted. The Northwestern Ohio Historical Society ascertained that the correct name of the fort was Miamis and not Miami (named for the river, once known as Miamis of the Lake); that the stockade was actually erected a short time before Wayne's arrival in the lower Maumee Valley; and that a 1796 itemized list of structures at the post included:

> *four bastions, a water battery, three bomb-proofs for soldiers' quarters, one bomb-proof for provision store and ordinance, one bunk house and oven, six log houses for officers' quarters, one guard house in the ditch, one blacksmith shop, [and] one carpenter shop.*

In addition to his inventory list, the recorder reported that the fort, less than two years old, was "very much out of repair." The decline continued unchecked in the 19th century. By the mid-20th century, a local journalist described the former fortification as a "brush-tangled scene," providing "a trysting place for lovers, a fishing scene . . . and a beach for occasional nude bathing parties."

Describing the Fort Miamis site of the 19th century in a 1944 article for the *Northwest Ohio Quarterly*, F. Clever Bald wrote, "Over the mounds that had once been glacis and ramparts, horses and cattle grazed. The stronghold, which had loomed so large in Governor Simcoe's martial plans, was all but forgotten."

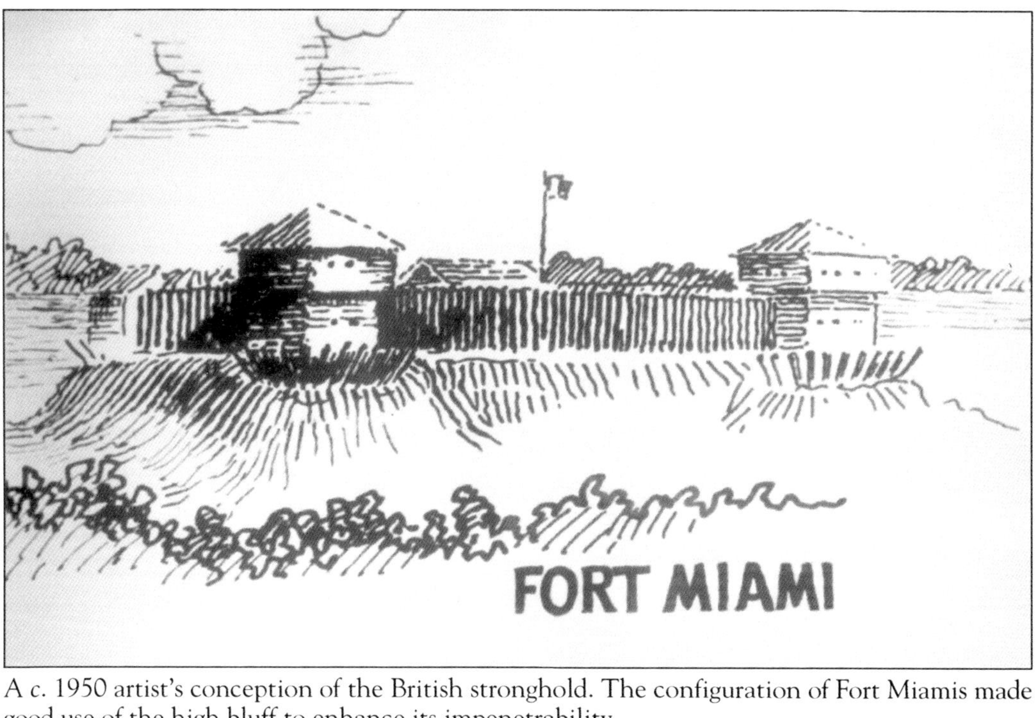

A *c.* 1950 artist's conception of the British stronghold. The configuration of Fort Miamis made good use of the high bluff to enhance its impenetrability.

Photograph of the earthworks at Fort Miamis, *c.* 1900. Note the cow on the horizon at right. (Courtesy of the Local History & Genealogy Department, Toledo-Lucas County Public Library.)

Both Turkey Foot Rock and Fort Miamis were regular stops along the "Pumpkin Vine," a branch of an interurban rail line that operated between Waterville and Maumee, 1901–1910. The amphibian passenger poked fun at the trolley's terminus, Frogtown (aka Toledo).

Fort Miamis became Port Miamis after the abandonment of the military post. Note the steamboat at left.

This sign indicates that historians of the early 20th century confused Maumee's Fort Miami(s) with an earlier Fort Miami(s) built in the upper valley, near present Fort Wayne.

The site of Fort Miamis became a popular retreat for city dwellers a century ago. Dr. G. Michael Pratt's archaeological excavation of Fort Miamis in the 1980s yielded a wealth of early 20th century debris left by picnickers.

A 1950s aerial view of old Fort Miamis. Traces of the ravelin (a V-shaped outwork between two bastions) can be seen at right-center. (Courtesy of *The Blade*, Toledo.)

This photograph was captioned, "Diggers at Fort Miamis Site." An archaeological excavation sponsored by the Anthony Wayne Parkway Board was under way by the autumn of 1953. (Courtesy of *The Blade*, Toledo.)

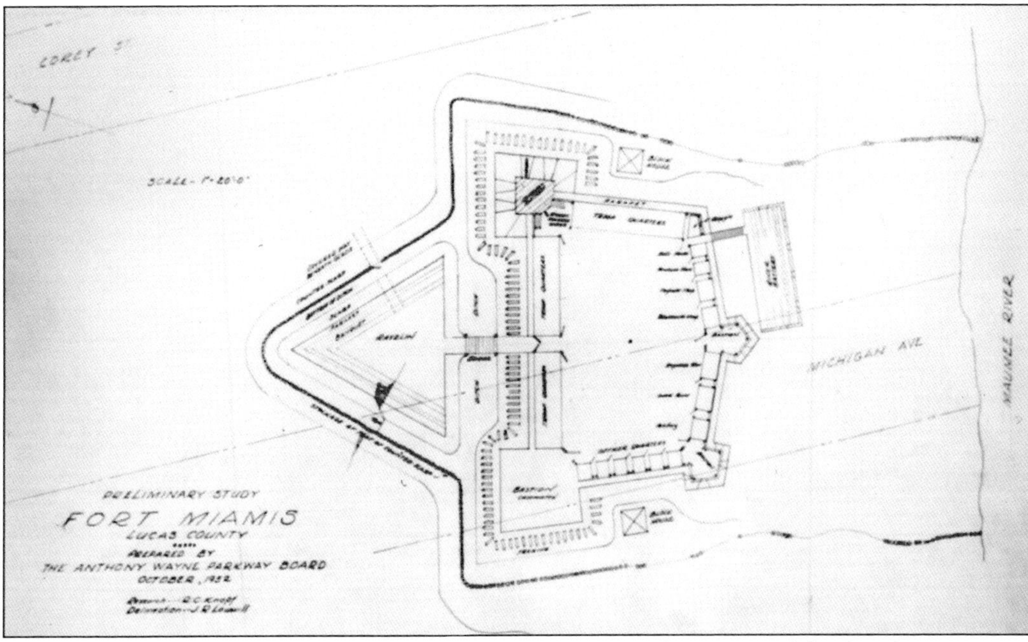

The archaeology aided in platting the late 18th century configuration of the fortification.

From left, Raymond Baby, archaeologist with the Ohio Historical Society; J.R. Lawrence Lawwill, director of anthropology with the Anthony Wayne Parkway Board; and Harold Peterson, chief of the historical branch of the National Park Service, convene at the site of Fort Miamis. Thought had been given to reconstructing the structure, *a la* Fort Meigs. (Courtesy of *The Blade*, Toledo.)

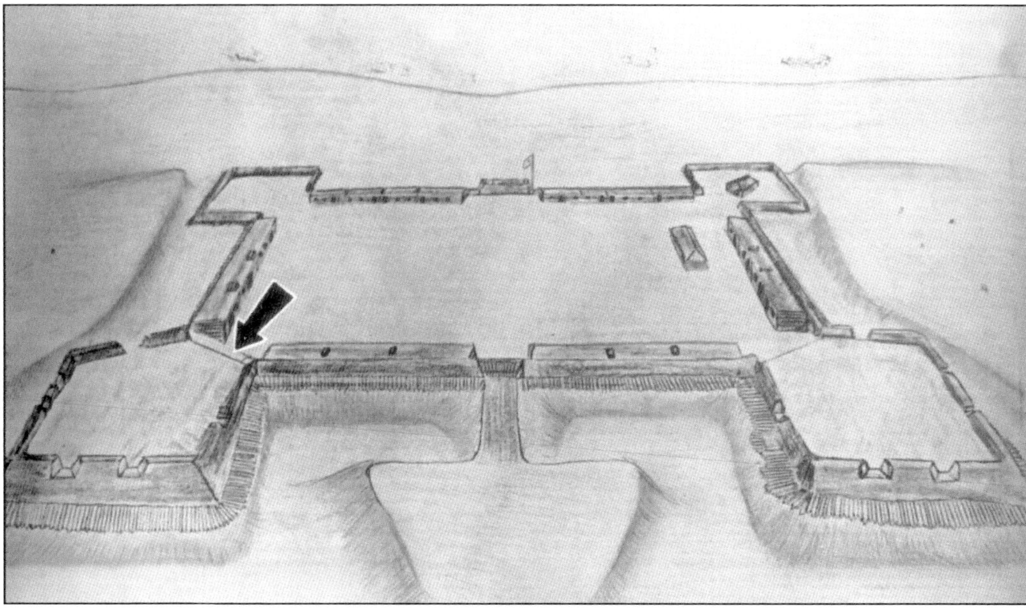

Another artist's conception of the fort, this one a three-dimensional perspective. The arrow indicates a bastion feature excavated by archaeologists. (Courtesy of *The Blade*, Toledo.)

A "digger" uncovers a 19th century feature, September 1953. (Courtesy of *The Blade*, Toledo.)

Another "digger" shows his finds, among them hand-forged nails and a prehistoric celt, to the photographer, September 1953. (Courtesy of *The Blade*, Toledo.)

Following the initial archaeological project, the Ohio Historical Society of Northwestern Ohio (the present Lucas County-Maumee Valley Historical Society), in cooperation with the Anthony Wayne Parkway Board, erected this marker along River Road, Maumee.

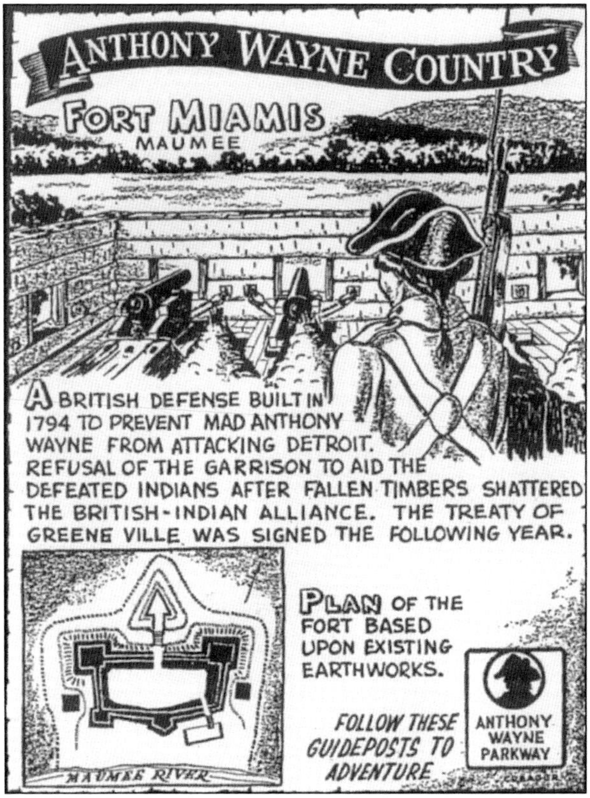

The Parkway Board included this cartoon synopsis in its 1950s *Anthony Wayne Country* "guide booklet."

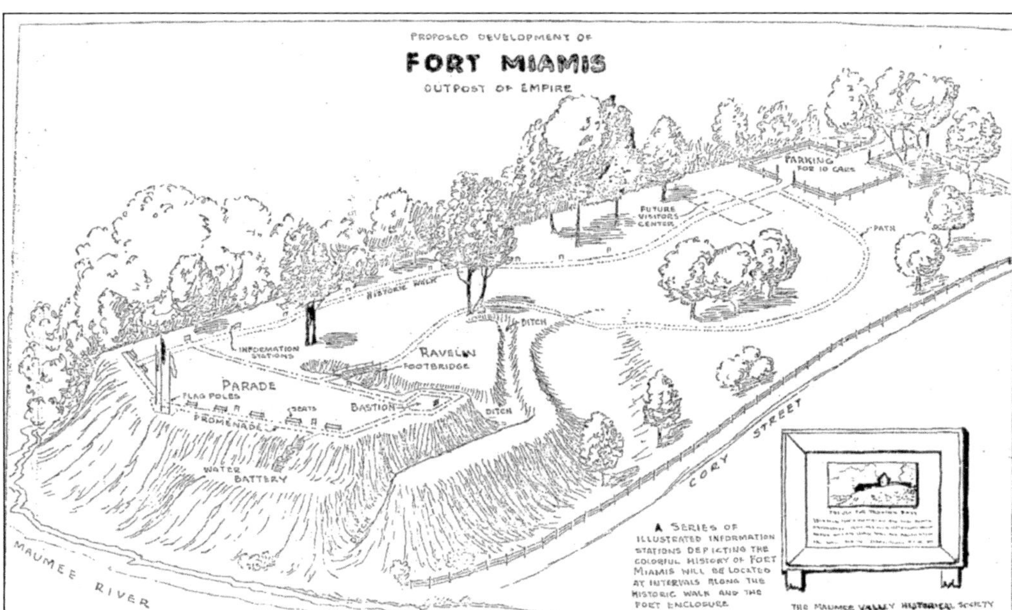

"Fort Miamis—Outpost for Empire" was the 1980s concept for an open-air museum proposed by the Maumee Valley Historical Society. The site remained largely undeveloped, much to the approval of winter sledders.

Dr. G. Michael Pratt of Heidelberg College followed up the 1950s archaeology with a major excavation three decades later. Here, his assistant points out a timber of Fort Miamis. (Courtesy of *The Blade*, Toledo.)

The "diggers" unearth additional timberwork. (Courtesy of *The Blade* of Toledo.)

A retrospective of Fort Maimis would not be complete without a reference to the Fort Miami Racetrack, built north by west of the outpost site at the Lucas County Fairground. A capacity crowd gathered for a 1957 horse race. (Courtesy of *The Blade*, Toledo.)

Down to the wire—a close finish in a 1950s race. (Courtesy of *The Blade*, Toledo.)

AND THEY'RE OFF!—the Fort Miami track also witnessed thrilling car races in the 1950s. (Courtesy of *The Blade*, Toledo.)

On his way to the winner's circle: a Fort Miami "speed demon," *c.* 1955. (Courtesy of *The Blade*, Toledo.)

End of an era: The raceway burned to the ground in 1957. There was actually a silver lining to the dark smoke clouds: The conflagration opened the way for a new recreational facility to be constructed. (Courtesy of *The Blade*, Toledo.)

Preliminary National Park Service plans call for a minimalist development of the current Fort Miamis Park.

A badge prepared by the National Park Service in anticipation of the opening of their "new" historic sites. (Courtesy of the National Park Service.)

The "oxbow" around McKee's Island provided a setting for the novel *Princess of Arcady*, published in 1900. It was co-authored by *Blade* city editor Arthur Henry and Theodore Dreiser. The latter went on to write *Sister Carrie* and *An American Tragedy*.

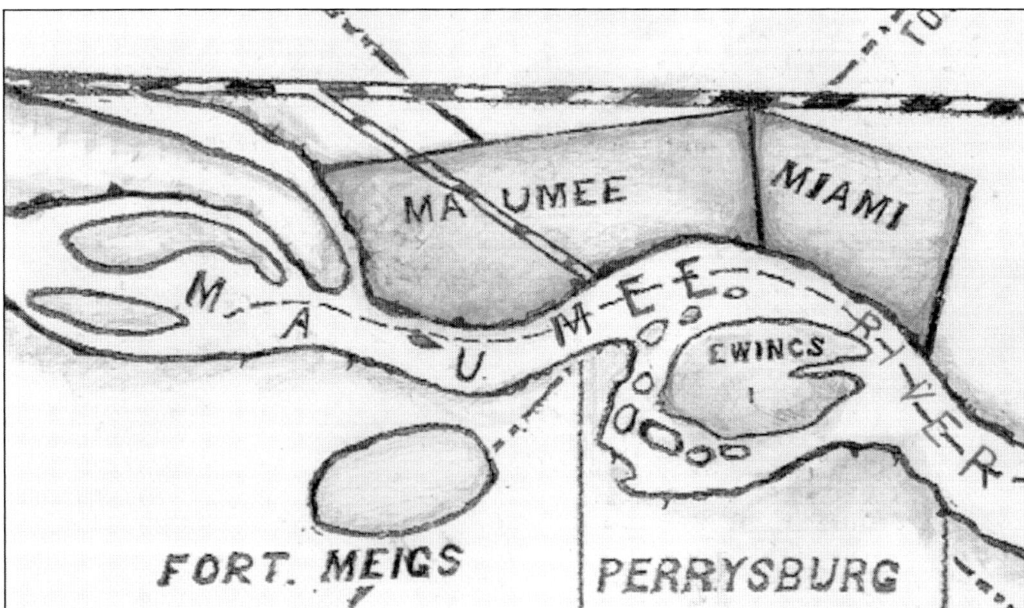

A sister city of Maumee, Miami City grew up around the ruins of the British fortification in the 1830s. The Port of Miami utilized the old anchorage, and a customs house was built just outside the earthworks. The son-in-law of Captain William Wells, Judge James Wolcott, was one of several investors in a suburban venture, and created a Wolcott's Addition on the west side of the settlement.

Eight

Fort Industry

In 1965, a cluster of eight plants took root in greater metropolitan Toledo, and "Fort Industry Industrial Park" was born. The name was a nod to the city's pioneer past and lasting legacy of enterprise.

In a similar vein, a century before, Jesup W. Scott proclaimed Toledo to be "The Future Great City of the World." He did more than any other local leader to publicize and promote the Lucas County seat while calling attention to the city's inspiring heritage. It was said that Scott, along with Anthony Wayne, best embodied the frontier spirit of the Maumee Valley.

In truth, Wayne held contempt for the lower Maumee valley and its pioneers. The Foot of the Rapids, Swan Creek, and other Anglo-Indian settlements were regarded as "nests of villainy." Contrary to popular belief, his Legion did not build the allegorical Fort Industry, but rather burned the region's log structures to the ground.

A scene from Downes' *The Conquest*. The vanquished warriors with their families assembled at the mouth of Swan Creek, making what is present downtown Toledo a vast camping ground and depot for the receipt of British supplies. McKee's auxiliaries failed to come through with the promised supplies, and, to quote Downes, "The poor huddled mass of half-starved humanity of Swan Creek became daily more willing to meet with Wayne as they became more wretched from hunger and disease."

Following the Battle of Fallen Timbers, a British official at the Foot of the Rapids reported that the Indians were "very low spirited and disheartened." This melancholic scene appeared in *Wayne's Peace with the Indians of the Old Northwest, 1795*, published by the Allen County Public Library, Fort Wayne, Indiana, in the early 1950s. (Courtesy of the Allen County Public Library.)

TOLEDO IN 1800

This is a conjectural picture reproduced from an old painting. In it Fort Industry appears as even more elaborate and substantial than in Colonel Hipkin's drawing. The best information is that the "fort" was little more than a mere stockade.

Read a plaque once placed on the corner of Monroe and Summit streets, Toledo, "Site of Fort Industry, a stockade erected by General Anthony Wayne, in the year 1794 as a safeguard against the British who then held Fort Miamis." Most early historians attributed Fort Industry to "Mad Anthony," and to this day, not a few residents of Lucas County associate the fortification with the Campaign of 1794.

A conjectural scene by O.J. Hopkins, 1873, entitled "Landing at Fort Industry (Toledo) of the First Continental Regiment of the United States Infantry Under Colonel Thomas Hunt, June 1803." Commented Van Tassel, "It was very unlikely that Fort Industry was as complete and elaborate and shown here." The local historian, however, confirmed that it did exist as a temporary outpost station in 1803, and that Hunt and his troops did indeed "disembark here on their way from Fort Niagara to Fort Wayne."

"There are No Luriking Indians in the Background" read the caption of this *Toledo Times* photograph published in 1937. This replica of Fort Industry was erected for the Toledo Centennial Celebration and served as a tourist information "headquarters." (Courtesy of the Local History & Genealogy Department, Toledo-Lucas County Public Library.)

"Frogtown" gave way to "Fort-town" in the 20th century. Toledo's finest wore this patch, *c.* 1950.

Fort Industry was adopted as a logo for the Toledo Centennial Celebration of 1937.

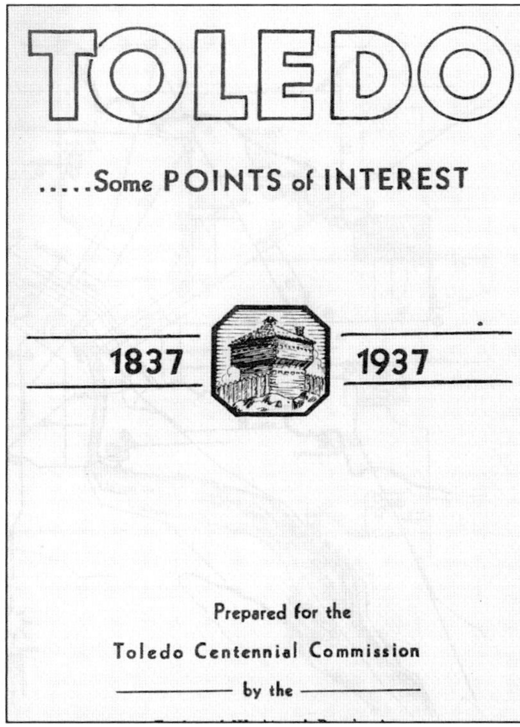

Fort Industry at Swan Creek provided the centerpiece of the Seal of the City of Toledo, *c.* 1940, rendered by Ernest Sprig. (Local History & Genealogy Department, Toledo-Lucas County Public Library.)

A more recent Seal of the City of Toledo reduced the Maumee Bay fortification to a blockhouse.

The Fort Industry Block was established at Monroe and Summit streets, Toledo, at the height of the Victorian Age. (Courtesy of the Local History & Genealogy Department, Toledo-Lucas County Public Library.)

A century later, entrepreneurs looked to revive the downtown with Fort Industry Square, per a promotional brochure, "a distinctive address in a quality business setting of tradition and charm found only in the 100 Block of Summit Street." (Courtesy of *The Blade*, Toledo.)

Mayor Doug Deford and downtown boosters Jeff Drake and Dr. Robert Hauman got the revitalization project "off the ground" in June of 1978. (Courtesy of *The Blade*, Toledo.)

"Time Marches On—4 Feet Sideways" was the original caption for this photograph. The 20-foot clock was originally installed in 1913 in front of the George Kapp Jewelry Store at 413 Summit Street. In 1980, it was acquired for Fort Industry Square. (Courtesy of *The Blade*, Toledo.)

Whites and Indians meet: this vintage relief at Fort Industry Square commemorated Columbus' first voyage to the New World and seems to make an oblique reference to Wayne's encounter with the Confederacy. (Courtesy of *The Blade*, Toledo.)

Per a 1970s promotional brochure, "The large Fort Industry Square parking lot offers ample parking space for tenants, shoppers, and clients coming to the square for business or pleasure." (Courtesy of *The Blade*, Toledo.)

Fort Industry Industrial Park was laid out in the early 1960s south from the Michigan-Ohio line to Matzinger Road, and west to east between Stickney Avenue and Hagman Road. Here Earl Cook, executive secretary for the Toledo Area Development Corporation, poses with a scale model. (Courtesy of *The Blade*, Toledo.)

It's a blast! In October of 1964, Ohio Governor Rhodes and Toledo Mayor Zuchowski helped depress the plunger that set off the first dynamite charge for the Fort Industry Industrial Park project. (Courtesy of *The Blade*, Toledo.)

The barren ground of the industrial park site was promoted as a fertile ground for "plants." As a publicity stunt, the TADC actually perched a woman with a watering can above the flower; newspaper page designers masked them out for the published photo. (Courtesy of *The Blade*, Toledo.)

Another publicity stunt: The TADC wanted to show prospective industrialists that their park was "corporate airplane friendly." (Courtesy of *The Blade*, Toledo.)

Nine

"We Will Make a New World"

In the fall of 1794, word reached the United States and Canada that Chief Justice John Jay's negotiations with the British had brought adjustment to "all matters in dispute." Great Britain agreed to withdraw from Fort Miamis and other ceded posts in American territory. Coupled with the defeat at the Battle of Fallen Timbers, the treaty was devastating to the Canadians and Indians; historian Wiley Sword (*President Washington's Indian War*, 1985) wrote that they suffered the "essence of despair."

The representatives of the federal government, on the other hand, were ebullient. They found their now-defeated and disenchanted enemy ready to make accommodations; a Chippewa chief told Wayne, "We will assist you to the utmost of our power to do what is right. . . . We will make a new world."

Affirmed John Tebbel, author of *The Battle of Fallen Timbers* (1972),

> *Indian resistance in the Old Northwest had ended, and it would never be so threatening again even under Tecumseh's leadership. The alliance between the British and the Indians, which had caused so much mischief, was broken and would not be renewed again until the War of 1812. Most important, from the standpoint of the American government, a new and fertile area had been cleared and made reasonably safe for settlement by the people of the expanding new nation.*

In a similar vein, the unnamed editor of Maumee's *Centennial History* (1938) made another reference to that "new and fertile area":

> *Vines of yesterday are trailing, seared and broken by the way; the luscious fruit today falls at our feet . . . the blossoms of tomorrow are but the embryo of a jungle yet untouched. . . . We take the stores of the past, which become the provender of the present and the cache of the future. . . . We are again on the trail, and life is on its way with us.*

A plaque on the base of the Wayne Monument documents that the Battle of Fallen Timbers culminated in the Greenville Treaty. (Courtesy of *The Blade*, Toledo.)

An Anthony Wayne Parkway promotion featured a scene adapted from a Howard Chandler Christy mural at the Ohio State Capitol. Wayne avowed to the followers of Little Turtle, "I now fervently pray to the Great Spirit that the peace now established may be permanent, and that it may hold us together in the bonds of friendship until time shall be no more."

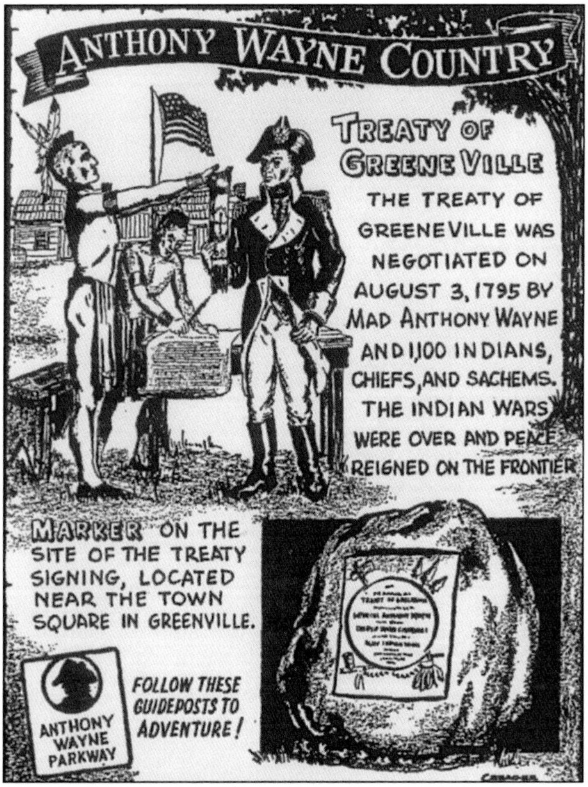

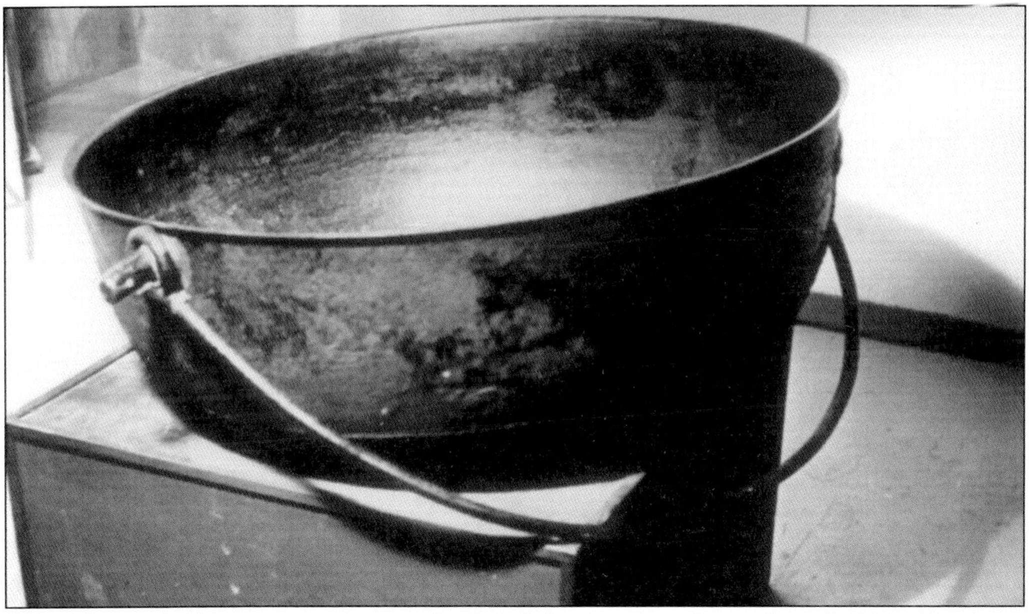

When "time shall be no more" came for "Mad Anthony" in December of 1796. The long-suffering general finally succumbed to gout and an intestinal disorder, and his corpse was temporarily interred under the blockhouse at Presque Isle, Erie, Pennsylvania. The remains were destined to be exhumed, carved up, and rendered in the kettle for ease of transport to a family plot in his native Keystone State. (Courtesy of *The Blade*, Toledo.)

Little Turtle, another sufferer of gout ("the well-to-do white man's infirmity"), survived long enough to see the hard-fought, hard-forged peace jeopardized by the gathering storm cloud of the War of 1812. He was buried not far from the headwaters of the Maumee River at Fort Wayne.

What well may be the likeness of Little Turtle, his son-in-law William Wells, and Anthony Wayne grace the front panel of the Maumee Valley Transportation Company's 1961 bus schedule. Note Turkey Foot Rock beneath the tree.

Both the Maumee Valley Transportation Company and the Anthony Wayne Parkway Board encouraged groups to "Charter a Bus" and follow the "Guideposts to Adventure."

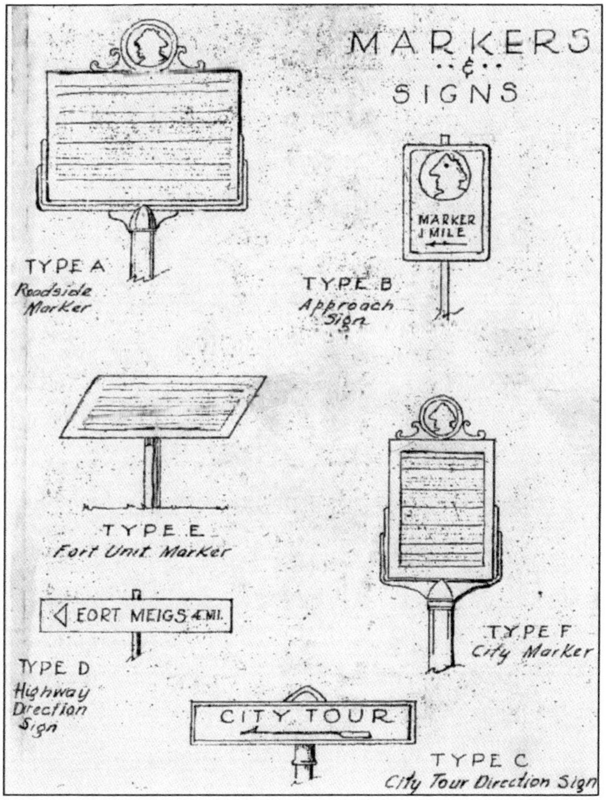

A 1940s Anthony Wayne Parkway Board included these schematics for roadside signage to promote heritage tourism.

A "ghostly" reminder of the old Anthony Wayne Trail (Parkway) is this faded sign in Waterville.

Many residents of Lucas County anticipated a postage stamp to mark the bicentennial of the Battle of Fallen Timbers. They had to settle for a commemorative cancellation authorized by the United States Postal Service.

These local Boy Scout badges reflect a youthful interest and pride in the heritage of Wayne's Trace.

Frontier Battle Fought Again

Fallen Timbers takes its place on the History Channel.

The assembled chiefs of the Indian Confederacy met to discuss strategy before the Battle (inset). Little Turtle (center) counseled for peace but was overruled.

It wasn't the right time or the right place, but if you know your history you'd have done a double take. You'd have sworn you were witnessing the Battle of Fallen Timbers. Only it wasn't 1794, it was a recent Saturday. The place wasn't the Maumee battlefield but a mature woodland at Secor Metropark that best represented what the battlefield must have looked like. The scene was repeated on Sunday at Fort Meigs, only the War of 1812 fort served as a stand-in for Fort Miamis, Fort Recovery and Fort Greenville. It was all staged for A&E/History Channel cameras in town to film action segments for a one hour program on the Battle of Fallen Timbers.

It was at Fallen Timbers in Maumee where an American Legion under the command of General "Mad Anthony" Wayne along with a contingent of Kentucky militia met and defeated a confederation of Native Americans. Wayne's victory in 1794 is sometimes referred to as the last battle of the Revolution because it resulted in securing the Northwest Territory, a five-state region that had not been ceded by the Indians. The brief battle was decisive in bringing the Indians to sign the

6

Treaty of Greenville in 1795, giving the United States control over portions of Ohio, Michigan, Indiana, Illinois and Wisconsin. Without the treaty, our area might have remained a buffer zone between Indian and settled territory or even become part of Canada.

Sixty actors or, more correctly, reenactors came from all over the Midwest to realistically portray Native Americans, Wayne's legion, the Kentucky volunteers, and Wayne's scouts. Two were local. Whitehouse resident Jared McKenzie portrayed William Wells, a white man raised as a Miami Indian. Sylvania native Craig Fisher played Anthony Wayne.

"We're here to create an accurate portrayal of the battle," Gary Foreman, series creator, producer and director, said. "Accuracy isn't limited to uniforms and attire, the background has to be accurate, too. We chose Secor because it's a mature American forest of the type that would have been found at Fallen Timbers. We're excited to tell an important story that's never been told on national television. Just as important, we're here to call attention to the effort to preserve the Fallen Timbers Battlefield."

It is Foreman's intention that the program be premiered locally and tied to the campaign to save the battlefield. Mr. Foreman is from Valparaiso, Indiana. The program is one of a four part series he's shooting that highlights decisive battles on the American frontier. Others in the series titled "FRONTIER: The Decisive Battles" will depict the Battle of King's Mountain, the Blackhawk War and the Battle of New Orleans. They are set to air on the History Channel either in late fall or in winter following the holidays.

General "Mad Anthony" Wayne, portrayed by Craig Fisher of Sylvania, gathers his dragoons. Director Gary Foreman (inset) ponders the arrangement of a scene.

7

The Battle of Fallen Timbers received national attention by way of a History Channel documentary that debuted in 1999. Gary Foreman, creator of the television series *FRONTIER: The Decisive Battles*, arrived at Secor Metropark, one of the Toledo Area Metroparks, with a film crew and told a reporter,

> *We're here to create an accurate portrayal of the battle. Accuracy isn't limited to uniforms and attire; the battleground has to be accurate, too. We chose Secor because it's a mature American forest of the type that would have been found at Fallen Timbers. We're excited to tell an important story that's never been told on national television. Just as important, we're here to call attention to the effort to preserve the Fallen Timbers Battlefield.* (Courtesy of the Metroparks of the Toledo Area.)

Marble statuary by Decoline, Ltd., of Whitehouse, Ohio, created this popular landmark that stands in front of the General's Chophouse Restaurant in Waterville, along the present Anthony Wayne Trail. The reverse of a bookmark featuring the statue reads,

> *Had it not been for Gen. Mad Anthony Wayne's Victory 1 mile east of Waterville at the Battle of Fallen Timbers (1794), the Western border of the United States probably wouldn't have made it past the Mississippi River. He is shown in this statute at about the age of 30.* (Courtesy of Decoline, Ltd.)

"Now I'm Really Mad." This bumper-sticker was created to help fight the Mall at Fallen Timbers, contiguous to the National Park Service historic site. It is the inspiration of Stop the Mall campaign coordinator Dave Westrick. The "Second Battle of Fallen Timbers," pitting developers and their disciples against citizens that have taken historic preservation to heart, has swung back and forth for half a decade. (Courtesy of Dave Westrick.)